that many of the anti-depressants available, were far less effective than previously thought and stopped doing research into depression!

Fortunately for us, Terrence Watts concluded there was another way to help sufferers. In this meticulously written book, Terrence Watts shows a deep personal understanding, as he 'takes on' this complex illness. Speaking as he would in one of his excellent training classes, the author effortlessly guides both the sufferer and the therapist through the 'mind-field' of issues: explaining in easily achievable exercises, how to 'take on' and to help overcome this illness.

John Bailey, Hypnotherapist, psychotherapist and councilor

If you – or anyone you care about – are experiencing depression, I urge you to read this extraordinary book. Written in friendly, no-nonsense language, *Smashing Depression* goes to the heart of the problem and offers clear and practical strategies for dealing with it. Essential reading for anyone struggling with depression – or anyone who cares about someone who is. Get it. Read it. Pass it on!

Peter Field, Hypnotherapist and Author of *The Chi of Change*

Having experienced depression some years ago without really knowing I was depressed until I got through it, a book like this would have been helpful as it explains depression and its effects. With the exercises to look at and shift your beliefs and behaviour patterns, it gives you the tools to help you move out of the dark and into the light. Though the book is aimed at depression I think it would also be useful when you find yourself stuck in a low mood or life is getting out of control, which could lead to depression. Using the tools can get you back on track creating healthy choices and changes before slipping further down. This book can help you to focus on creation and choice as opposed to reaction and limitation which can take away your power and limit choices. I now help clients with depression and would recommend this book as a useful tool to use between sessions.

Pete Bateman, Hampshire Hypnotherapy

Smashing Depression

Escaping the Prison and Finding a Life

Smashing Depression

Escaping the Prison and Finding a Life

Terence Watts

**PSYCHE
BOOKS**

Winchester, UK
Washington, USA

First published by Psyche Books, 2014
Psyche Books is an imprint of John Hunt Publishing Ltd., Laurel House, Station Approach,
Alresford, Hants, SO24 9JH, UK
office1@jhpbooks.net
www.johnhuntpublishing.com
www.psyche-books.com

For distributor details and how to order please visit the 'Ordering' section on our website.

Text copyright: Terence Watts 2014

ISBN: 978 1 78279 619 0

A CIP catalogue record for this book is available from the British Library.

Design: Lee Nash

Printed and bound by CPI Group (UK) Ltd, Croydon, CR0 4YY

We operate a distinctive and ethical publishing philosophy in all
areas of our business, from our global network of authors to
production and worldwide distribution.

CONTENTS

There are four stages to learning anything and that includes how to be depressed... as well as how to escape. Discover the importance of the PPF test.

There's still a little work to do but just as in all the best stories, the most exciting bit happens towards the end. The real you is now beginning to awaken.

The stage is set, all the props are in place and you are now just about ready to fully join the show that is 'Life' – and this section will complete the task.

In this final part of the book, you learn how to keep and build on the changes you've made – and also how to develop a 'first aid kit' for emergencies.

This book is dedicated to my lovely wife
Julie
without whom my life might be depressing

Foreword

by Dr. Rafiq Lockat

I first heard Terence Watts' name when I attended an advanced hypnotherapy course some years ago. The presenter made reference to some of his work in hypnosis. He also made reference to several other experts in the course, but for some reason Terence Watts stuck in my head . Later I googled him and discovered his inspiring website, "Hypnosense".

I purchased some of his books and it was then that I realized why I had been attracted to his work at that training course: his clarity of thought; elegance of expression and ability to take proven concepts and adapt them to ingenious new therapeutic techniques were ground breaking.

I have been a Clinical Psychologist for 24 years, and I can say without hesitation that using the tools Terence provided in the material I purchased, transformed my clinical practice. My psychotherapy sessions decreased and the results were significantly more effective. After a short while I became a fan of Terence Watts' work. Over time Terence and I became acquainted with each other's work and a mutual respect and friendship developed.

But enough about us. Let's get down to the reason you purchased this book... depression.

Depression is a common mental disorder that presents with feelings of guilt or low self-worth, loss of interest or pleasure, decreased energy, , disturbed sleep or appetite, depressed mood, and poor concentration. Moreover, depression often comes with symptoms of anxiety. These problems can become chronic or recurrent and lead to substantial impairments in an individual's ability to take care of his or her everyday responsibilities. At its worst, depression can lead to suicide.

According to the World Health Organisation (WHO), depression affects over 350 million people worldwide (that's more than the entire population of the USA. Other research shows that 1 in 4 people in the UK suffers from depression. Depending on the number and severity of symptoms, depression can be categorized as mild, moderate or severe. The WHO also lists preferable treatment options for depression as consisting of basic psycho-social support combined with anti-depressant treatment and psycho-therapy. However it also states that medication should not be the first line of treatment for mild or sub-threshold depression. As an adjunct to care by specialists and primary healthcare, self-help is listed as an important approach to helping people with depression. Self-help books have been shown to reduce and treat depression in numerous studies in Western countries (Andrews et al. 2011).

So this is where Terence's book comes in. It is a self-help book about overcoming mild to moderate depression. During my 10 years as a Senior Academic in the Department of Psychology at the University of the Western Cape in Cape Town, I have reviewed several books, book chapters and journal articles and I can comfortably state that this book, Smashing Depression, is the most user-friendly one I have ever come across. Terence's trademark style of cutting out the fat to get to the meat is evident throughout the book. What Terence has done is to gather his 24 years of experience, wisdom and unique insights into mental health and condensed them into this brilliant book. He has written it in a simple, but not simplistic, style and stripped all the jargon so beloved of other 'experts' in the field. At times he is gentle and persuasive and, where appropriate, confrontational and challenging in order to get the reader to understand and change those stubborn patterns that keep them 'locked in' to the depressive mode. He has utilized exciting and thought-provoking questionnaires as well as easy to use techniques to keep the readers' interest focused on themselves and therefore focused on the changes that are necessary for success.

So, I have no doubt that everyone who reads this book with an open mind will derive enormous benefit from Terences's special insights. Depression is like falling into a deep, dark hole with no obvious way out. This book offers the ladder to climb out into the bright sunlight.

Rafiq Lockhat
Clinical Psychologist (M.A. (Clin Psych) Natal)
Former Vice Chairperson: South African Society of Clinical Psychologists
Executive Member: Psychological Society Of South Africa. Cape Town

Preface

A message from the Author

This is no ordinary book about how to get out of the depression trap. I'm not a medical practitioner of any sort and I don't have a string of university degrees after my name. What I am is a successful therapist who has been working with people, using *their* language to help them deal with *their* fears, *their* hopes... and *their* depressions. This is something that I've been doing since 1989 and also something I've been successfully teaching other therapists to do in my own training school since 1999.

I wrote this book after being told several times by clients and students that they had read several works on depression and how to get free from it, but that they all seemed rather impersonal. They somehow missed the important point that people suffering from depression don't want jargon and theory; it doesn't really help much to be told that depression affects mostly the strongest minds and some very famous people. What they need is something they can easily understand without the aid of a dictionary and a thesaurus, something that is written in everyday language, and includes easy-to-understand exercises that help to make real and lasting change.

Well, this is it...

Terence Watts, 2014

The First Step

Getting started on getting you fixed

It is vital that you have consulted with a doctor about being depressed before beginning any self-help programme.

The problem with depression is that it's an illness which can be self-defeating... unless you can manage to effectively use one or more of the following: *an 'act of will', self-persuasion, honest experiment, self-questioning, physical change, reality checks, acceptance* and any of the other ideas – some of them unique – presented in this book. Get a good hold of just *one* of those easy-to-learn concepts well enough to use it and your life will start to improve. Definitely. Understand and use *more* than one and you'll be truly amazed at the changes you can make.

The most important thing is to recognise that if you can remember a time when you felt either more depressed or less depressed than you do now, then *change* is not only possible but probable. The trick is to make that change go in the right direction, and that's where this book comes in. It's often been said that the longest of journeys starts with just a single step... but the most important thing to be sure of is that all the steps that follow go in the same direction.

So let's get started!

Chapter One

I shouldn't feel like this!

DISCLAIMER: This depression relief programme is not intended to replace any medication or conventional treatment/therapy. It is designed specifically to work with individuals suffering relatively mild depression who are still able to function on a day-to-day basis, albeit while having to make considerable physical and emotional effort to do so. It is not suitable for those who suffer from bi-polar disorder, psychosis-related depressions, or the group of disorders classified as Major Depression.

Most people who know depression will have said: *'I shouldn't feel like this...'* far more times than they can remember – and if that includes you, then you are absolutely right!

So let's start by stating an absolute fact right from the beginning, and that is that you really don't have to stay the way you are. It *is* a matter of choice even if it doesn't feel like it. The solution to the problem lies in discovering the right tools to do the job – after all, if somebody didn't know a saw existed they'd make a pretty poor show of trying to fell a tree. They might even decide it was altogether impossible and give up. Now, the good news is that *you* haven't given up or you wouldn't be wasting your time reading this book. It might be that you don't so much *know* there's an answer somewhere as *hope* there is... Well, that's okay, too, because there is, and you're holding it right now!

One thing that is important before we go any further is to ensure that you have had a blood test to see if you are deficient in Vitamin B12 – many people are, without knowing it, and might dismiss their symptoms as being associated with work issues or some other type of stress. The fact is, though, that shortage of this essential vitamin in your blood can cause all sorts of psychological ills, including:

- Depression
- Anxiety
- Insomnia
- Irritability
- Paranoia
- Delusions

It's more common in people over fifty years old and/or those on a vegan or vegetarian diet. It's not covered in a standard blood test and it is a fact that many doctors will prescribe anti-depressants without even considering a blood test. You can actually be low on B12 for years with no symptoms at all until the level finally drops below the minimum for proper physical and mental heath. So if the depression you suffer seemed to come on rather suddenly and you have no idea as to the cause of it, do take a trip to the doctor and ask to be tested for B12 deficiency. Ignored, it can lead to Dementia and even Cancer...

Okay, that's the end of the physical health warning (though you might also want to get checked for other vitamin deficiencies as well.) Now, apart from the Vitamin B12 issue, there are one or two other important considerations to take into account about the nature of depression. There are actually two different types or 'styles' (actually, there are more than that but for the purposes of this programme, it is convenient to recognise just two.) They are:

- **Reactive:** Something has created the depressed state and even if you don't know what it is, you can probably remember when it started. It can almost always be lifted and this book is likely to do just that.
- **Endogenous:** This feels as if it's somehow 'built in' to your psyche (that's a posh way of saying your 'mind and personality'.) It's been there a long time and doesn't change much, either for the better or worse. It can improve greatly but may not lift altogether.

Generally speaking, neither type is totally constant but varies in its intensity. There are times when it is more tolerable than usual and other times when it seems as if life is barely worth carrying on with... and yet here you are, hoping against hope that something can set you free. It all means you're still looking for answers and this gives you much more chance of discovering what you need than if you were sitting down with your eyes closed. Of course, you have to know what sort of thing you're looking for in the first place and that's where this book comes in. It will help you discover how you can actually choose to be different and use the right tools to make the changes happen, tools that you might not realise even exist at this stage.

First, though, we're going to have a look, in no particular order, at some of the most common causes of depression. That way, you'll gather a bit of an understanding about it and when you properly understand something, you tend to fear it less and be more constructive. Just what we need! It's not all doom, either, because in Chapter Two, we're going to set about making some early changes upon which we can build later on.

Don't own it!

It's quite an amazing fact of life that most people will seek to own that which they really do not want! They talk about 'my' *depression, anxiety, nerves, insomnia* or whatever – and they do the same thing with even quite serious physical illnesses. When you think about it, the human animal is an acquisitive being and once we own something we tend to try to hang on to it – because the physical brain (it's often referred to as 'the subconscious' but sometimes in this book we're going to call it the brain – you'll see why later) recognises a pattern. The pattern is a simple one. When you talk about 'my' anything, the brain will start to do all sorts of little tricks in the background, tricks you don't even notice because they last for about one gazillionth of a second. They are designed to make you watchful in case you lose whatever you have just referred to... And it does that *especially* with depression! That might not make sense yet but it will later, so just for the moment try to accept that it is so.

Let's just think about the brain for a couple of moments. It's an amazing instrument, more complex than anything that can be created by man. It works at lightening speed and constantly monitors our surroundings for perceived danger. Parts of it have much more to do with balance and temperature control and a whole host of other essential 'housework and maintenance' tasks but we're not enormously interested in those at the moment. What we're interested in is that pattern recognition process. When you say 'my' anything the brain perceives it as an important part of you and therefore essential for survival... you might be way ahead of what you're reading now! The brain won't readily let go of anything that is important for you to survive. It's not a reasoning device, nor does it judge what you really mean very well, if at all... It simply recognises and acts upon patterns. Okay, there is *a lot* more to the brain than that but for our purposes here, that's the process you need to grasp.

So what if from this moment onwards, you always refer to depression as 'this depression' (avoid adding 'of mine') instead of 'my depression'? Now the brain recognises a different pattern altogether; it recognises that the depression is an external force or process, instead of a part of you that has to be guarded. This gives you a much better chance of getting rid of it! So where you might have said in the past: *"If it wasn't for **my** depression I could do so much more..."* you can now say instead: *"If it wasn't for **this** depression, I could do so much more..."* Maybe you can already feel how just that tiny change begins to put some distance between you and it...

Just checking...

It might come as something of a surprise to realise that it's not unusual for somebody to believe they're depressed, when in reality they're experiencing something else. Here's a list of 'impostors':

- Unhappy
- Fed up
- Stressed
- Anxious
- Plain bored

Those all have similar components to depression but usually differ in one important specific facet – sudden variability. In each of those cases, it's entirely possible for events and happenings to trigger a sudden lift of mood to at least an acceptable level. But when the depression is real, the emotional responses themselves are depressed and almost completely inactive or dormant.

So, if you've just discovered that you're actually not depressed at all but suffering one of the other problems, put this book down at once! Perhaps do some retail therapy.

Okay, so you're still here... and now you know what you're getting to grips with so we can really get down to work. See if you can answer this question: *"Why are you depressed anyway?"* This is a 'vertical descent' approach and can sometimes take people to the very core of their problems. Just let your mind run with it for a few moments without trying too hard to think of an answer. There's no need to rush. Consider all the possibilities, even the ones you feel you really couldn't ever talk about. Perhaps you're not happy with your partner but they're a 'lovely person' and you can't bear to hurt them... Or maybe they treat you badly and you're frightened of them. It could be that your sex-life is rubbish but you just can't discuss it; you might be stuck with a habit that you loathe or an urge of some sort that is socially unacceptable. Whatever it is, if you know why you're depressed, it won't go away until you do something about it – and this book might not help as much as it would if you still needed to find something directly related to the cause of the depression.

We'll assume for the moment that you don't really know exactly why you're depressed – you just find yourself in that same same cold grey place that is the world and for the life of you can't see why some people are so damned happy!

Common concepts

We'll have a look at five of the common mental processes that so often lurk in the background of the depressed person's mind. It's odds on that at least one of these will resonate slightly with you and any one of them can quickly give way to new ideas. They are:

- Fear of death
- Karma – the 'what goes around comes around' concept
- Being a 'waste of space'
- Being an 'oxygen thief'
- Being 'Weird'

Of course, it might be that you're now shaking your head and musing that none of these is anything to do with you. Well, if so, congratulations! It means that the type of depression you are experiencing will almost certainly give way at some point, whether it's because of something in this book or just an odd 'bit of life' that suddenly makes a difference.

Anyway, we'll have a quick look at each of those things...

Fear of death

For some people, the knowledge that they will one day be no more is mind-numbingly frightening. For others, it's something that they almost look forward to, as an escape from the trials and tribulations of living. For yet others, the knowledge that all their striving is going to end in only one way is the source of a heavy depression. If this is you, then ask yourself which part of death it is that depresses/frightens you: *death itself, dying, being dead, or oblivion.*

For most people with this fear, it's the fourth one, oblivion. And yet we don't *know* that death results in oblivion. In fact, people who have experienced an NDE – a Near Death Experience – would insist that this is definitely not the case. (And you just try to change their mind. It can't be done!) And you can probably see that if we remove the idea of oblivion, then the whole death thing takes on a different and less scary or depressing 'slant'.

Take a moment or two to think about the part of you that you call 'I' or 'Me' when you're referring to yourself. You can think of it as your soul, essence, spirit or whatever else seems to work for you. Where does that part of you 'live' in your body? It might be your head, your heart or torso, maybe in an aura that somehow surrounds you... but wherever it is, it is a non-physical part of self. A surgeon couldn't remove it and examine it. A purely logical scientist will tell you it's just an illusion, the sum total of your life experiences to date. They assert that an NDE is just an hallucination created by the dying brain... Until they have one themselves! In 2012, a surgeon (very dismissive of NDEs are surgeons, as a rule) experienced just such an event for himself and has now come to the conclusion that awareness survives after death, at least for some time.

So how does this feel as you think about it? If the thought fills you with despair that even death won't allow you to escape from yourself, then this book might have been written especially for you. On the other hand, if it 'lifts' you a little, then be prepared to be lifted some more very soon.

And here's something that is interesting for many people: most depression depends upon the lives that others are leading, or are appearing to lead. It might be caused by a sense of unfairness of some sort, since it has been reported that in the UK during the Second World War, cases of depression being presented at doctors' surgeries dropped by 90%! Of course, everybody was in the same boat and one person's life wasn't so very much better than another's then... Though it might have just been the fact that people accepted depression as part of the war and believed it was 'normal' and therefore there was nothing to be done about it. Not by a doctor, anyway.

Karma

To some, it seems that they must surely be punished for something they've done in a past life and so the depression is a punishment and cannot be lifted. Or perhaps they feel it was something they've done in this life. We're not going into a big discussion on reincarnation or karmic debt here but suffice to say the argument doesn't really make any logical sense. The only reason it might carry some weight is if you believe it does. *Nobody is 'jinxed' for any reason whatsoever!* In fact, you can easily find awful people living a good life and the descendants of tyrants having a whale of a time! Now, if you feel that some Karmic influence is the cause of your problems, consider this idea: What if the only reason you're depressed is because you *believe* it's brought about by Karma and therefore inescapable? Try a little 'thought experiment'... Imagine, as vividly as you can, that you've just been absolved of all responsibility from everything any of your ancestors have done as well as from anything you've done (even if you can't remember anything bad.) The slate is wiped clean; pristine and unsullied. You have a chance to start again.

If that changes the way you feel, then you are able to do something totally amazing right at this moment. That totally amazing something is to recognise and accept that while you certainly can't 'unhappen' anything, you jolly well *can* set about making the world a better place in order to make amends! Learning how to let go of the depression will be the first step... Will you take it?

Waste of Space

This is usually the result, rather than the cause, of depression though it can easily feel as if it's the other way round. It's an odd phrase as well, when you think about it, too, since nobody can truly be a 'waste of space' – what would go in your space instead that would be better? Another person? Well, there's still enough space for everybody and everything, currently, and will be for many years to come. So it's just an empty saying and carries no meaning at all, in that case. It encourages depression to stick, though, unless you do something clever with it. *CHALLENGE IT!*

Challenge it and stop saying it! It's a fact that every time you think or speak of yourself in this way, you are programming your psyche to go ever deeper into depression. But think about the truth of it for a moment or two and ask yourself it it's truly possible for anybody to be a genuine 'waste of space'. It's nothing more than an insult that somebody created once and it's found its place with many people ever since as a 'humorous' remark; but if it *were* possible to be a 'waste of space' who comes closest? The person it was aimed at or the one being dismissively sarcastic?

Of course, the phrase isn't really meant literally – it's just intended to make somebody feel completely useless and unworthy. And it's a fact that *every single one of us* will be thought of in those terms at some point in our lives. But all it tells us is what the person doing the thinking is thinking! It's their thoughts only and of no more consequence than if they were claiming you were anything else that you actually are not.

If you bought a new jacket and one person said: *"That makes you look really cool!"*; then another said: *"Well, it's a bit average..."*; and a third person said: *"You look a right idiot!"* you might believe the third one automatically. But the jacket and you were the same all along, so those people weren't telling you anything about you, only about what they thought. And that's the way it is when anybody says anything about you. They are simply telling you what *they* think... and what they think is based on *their* lives and ideas and not yours.

Oxygen thief

This is exactly the same as 'Waste of Space' and you should treat it in the same way. The expression comes from somebody seeking to be amusing at the expense of somebody who they view as inferior for some reason. But we only attack that which we fear or don't understand, so the expression says far more about them than the person they were trying to demean.

Weird

Actually, everybody is weird! All 'weird' means in this context is 'different' and everybody is different from everybody else. So if somebody decides you're weird and chooses to say so, what they mean is that they don't understand you... So here we are back to people talking about themselves again and not about you! Right now, you might be thinking something along the lines of *'but everybody thinks I'm weird!'* But think about this. Do people who don't know you think you're weird? Does everybody recognise you as 'weird' immediately they meet you without you saying or doing anything? You might believe they do and if so, that's the cause of a lot of your problems...

If you truly believe you are weird, you will behave awkwardly around people because you're so sure they're going to think you're weird. And because you behave awkwardly you will seem... well... weird. But if you were to put on an act of being totally at ease with yourself, looking totally 'normal' people would think nothing of it at all. Well, they might envy you, especially if they think they're weird. (Actually, many people do but they tend to keep quiet about it!)

Making a start

Right, it's about time we started to do a bit of work that's designed to help you make a start on leaving depression behind you and finding a good life. Now, one of the most important things about all this is that there is *nothing in the world* that can get rid of the depression without your contribution to the task. There's not a self-help book, therapist, psychiatrist, guru, mystic, healer, magical fountain, grotto, river, sea or website or anything else that can work some miracle cure. Forget that whole idea of some mystical cure that you are just unable to access and you will become more receptive to *possible* ways of getting better... But you have to participate. Even if you go on medication, you have to remember to take the medicine in the first place. That's the bad news. The good news is that you're about to discover that participation is easy! So here's the first exercise to get you started on your way – it's not a permanent 'fix', just a permanent foundation to the work you're going to do later on. And foundations are everything, so do take it seriously.

*Imagine that you're standing in front of an old-fashioned double-sided full-length mirror on a stand (they're called a 'Cheval Mirror' by the way.) Imagine looking at your reflection, seeing yourself as you believe the world sees you. Whatever you think about what you can see in the reflection is fine – even if you think you look weird! Stay with it until any uncomfortable feelings begin to fade (it's quite normal to feel a bit uncomfortable at this stage.) As soon as the feelings start to fade – and they most definitely will because the physical brain cannot sustain the same stimulus forever – imagine reaching out with your toe and tipping the bottom of the mirror so that the whole thing swings over. Now you have to use your imagination because this side of the mirror shows the version of you that you really want to present to the world. It still looks like you physically, but you look great! You look **alive!** Don't do any 'ah buts' or 'yes buts' because this is just a mental* *game and you haven't got to make any changes that anybody will notice. Yet. Make it vivid in your mind and be sure to imagine yourself looking the way you would make yourself look if you could – and you can be as outrageous or as conservative, as 'posh' or as 'cool' as you choose. Keep looking until it starts to be difficult to keep the image in your mind then just stop thinking about the mirror for a moment or two. Instead, close your eyes and count slowly to ten. When you open your eyes again, see the mirror on the first side, let any discomfort fade (there will probably be less this time) then tip it over again, as you did before. Repeat this, including the eyes closed count of ten, a few times until you discover that the image of you that you would like to show the world starts to feel as if it really is a part of you. (Actually, it is!) That's when the exercise is complete for the time being.*

It's a good idea for you to repeat the exercise on a daily basis – it doesn't take very long and every time you do it you are chipping away at that negative image of yourself. What is most important to understand is that the 'good' image you created of yourself is potentially how you can become. It really *is* a part of the 'real you', even if that seems rather silly at the moment, because it's the product of your mind and nobody else's. You created it from the thought processes that are already there in the depths of your subconscious, so we'll finish this chapter with a phrase that is used and accepted by successful people and therapists all over the world:

If you can see it you can be it!

Chapter Two

Some questions and a surprise...

There are quite a few awkward questions that will be asked in this programme but don't be put off – and don't be tempted to skip the tough ones! In fact, don't be tempted to skip any of them if you're determined to get the best out of this book. If any of them should prove difficult for you to answer, this is a good thing, because it means you are being taken into parts of your mind that you don't normally visit. That's a vital part of any therapy or self-help process so it's fair to say that whenever you find a question you can't answer immediately, that's another step on the road to recovery. It's also worth the recognition that turning away from something in the past may have a bearing on the reason for the depression in the first place.

Anyway, on with some of the questions. You might find it a bit heavy going some of the time at first but keep focussed and you'll discover that it's actually easier than you thought. You don't have to answer everything at once, but you should make sure you finish each questionnaire before moving on to the next ones in the later chapters. In this one, choose as many answers as you like that seem to be part of how you 'work'.

Questionnaire One

Score every element on a 0 – 5 (5 high) basis that applies to the statement: *"I am depressed because..."*

1. I'm no longer young
2. I hate my face
3. My health is poor
4. I hate my body
5. I hate my family

6. I'm in debt
7. My house is a mess
8. My sex-life is rubbish
9. I feel like I'm a failure
10. I have relationship problems

What does it mean?

Questions 1 – 5 are about things that cannot be changed, while 6 – 10 are about aspects of life that *can* be changed, even though it might be difficult to do so. Now, for every '0' score, remove that statement and replace it with anything else you can think of that *does* have a score, being careful to keep it in the same group of 'can't be changed' or 'can be changed'. If you do remove a question and can't think of anything to replace it with, that's fine – just keep whatever's left. Now:

(a) Add the scores on questions 1 – 5: ____
(b) Add the scores on questions 6 – 10: ____

Depending on the balance of those two scores, it's possible to decide the best way to start working at lifting the depressed feeling as soon as possible – and as you start to feel better, so you will be able to function more comfortably and make even greater improvements to the way you feel. *And by the way, if you answered everything with a '5' you might need a bit of a rethink!* Anybody whose answers were *genuinely* all at a '5' level would almost certainly not be reading this book. They would in all probability be suffering an incapacitating **Lethargic Depression** in which they see no point in even thinking about how to get better. But you're reading this book... so you *are* thinking about getting better!

In other words, it's important that all the questionnaires are answered as accurately as possible if you are to get the best result from this book. And on that point, yes it **is** possible to get better with just the seven stages of the programme, though that doesn't necessarily means you have to do them all within a certain time of each other (though it would be best to keep them fairly close together.) It will depend on many factors, including how deep your depression 'sits' in your mind and how much time you have to work. The book is laid out in seven complete steps and the work in each can be completed in a single day if you have the time. But you might not want to complete the seven steps one after the other, preferring to go at a more leisurely pace and work through the exercises as and when you feel like it. Whatever works for you is the best thing for you. If you try to force the issue, all that is likely to happen is that you will become despondent because 'it' isn't working as fast as you want it to and you might then decide to give up. And that *definitely* won't get you to where you want to be, will it?

So, on to the scores now... If answer (a) is greater than answer (b) then you will need to work at **Acceptance,** which we'll look at in a moment or two. If, on the other hand, answer (b) is greater than answer (a) then you have to find a way of instigating **Change** and we'll soon get onto that, too. If both scores are the same, then start to work at Acceptance first.

Before we look at each of those concepts in some detail, though, there's something else to consider, concerning your underlying instinctive response to challenge. The good news is that you can pretty much choose how to use it, though one way will seem more familiar to you than the other. There are only two possible responses: **Active** and **Reactive.** Most of the time, you don't have to look too closely to see which of those states is operating, or to see which is the best one to use. Here are two friends – we'll call them Jane and Alice – responding differently to the situation where something uncomfortable has happened:

Jane: *"Oh no! This is disastrous! Why on earth does this sort of thing always happen to me? God knows how I'm supposed to get anywhere..."*

Alice: *"Oops! That wasn't supposed to happen! Okay, there's got to be a good way for me to deal with this..."*

You can easily see that Jane is *reactive* and merely drawing attention to what has gone wrong, perhaps looking for support and/or attention (more about *that* another time!). Alice, on the other hand, has recognised that something is not right with her plan and straight away becomes *active*, starting to search for a solution. It is a fact that depression tends to steer people towards being reactive rather than active; it's another fact that they can learn to recognise it, get a grip of it, and simply decide to be more constructive about the situation they find themselves in. It's fair to say that being reactive will never set you free from depression, the reasons for which will become obvious later, while an active state provides at least a *chance* of a massive improvement in your life.

You might well have discovered that you are by nature an automatically reactive type – well, good, if so you've just discovered one of the things you need to change in order to find a better life. Now you know what it is you can begin to get to it. If you discovered, though, that you are already an active responder (and there's no point claiming to be so if it isn't really the case) then that's also good – it's going to be even easier for you to get a good result from this programme.

Acceptance

Lack of acceptance causes pain, there's no doubt about that. Psychological or emotional discomfort is usually classified as 'pain' where the workings of the mind are concerned, so depression definitely qualifies. In this case, then, you can consider that lack of acceptance is going a long way towards causing or sustaining the depression. And if you have a high score at (a) and a low score at (b) then the work here is going to pay great dividends in no time at all.

You might be wondering how on earth you can be active instead of reactive when working at acceptance. Well, that's easy to answer:

- *The active response means working at accepting, letting go, and looking forward to being free from what feels bad*
- *The reactive response is to experience the pain and just complain about it without actually doing anything to feel better*

Nobody can *make* you accept anything. It has to come from inside you and in the next chapter you'll discover why that can sometimes be a little on the difficult side. But if you want to get better and get some fun out of life – and you *can* do that – then active acceptance is an essential behaviour.

Here's a simple little tale, again featuring our friends Jane and Alice, which illustrates the power of active acceptance. They've both lost a boyfriend and both are very sad.

Jane keeps on calling him but he tells her he's with someone else now. She refuses to give up hope and keeps on thinking about the life they had and desperately wants to get back with him. He stops returning her calls and she becomes steadily more miserable.

Alice calls him and asks him if he thinks he'll ever come back. He says he's with someone else now and she recognises it's final. She decides that although it's painful, she'd better just accept that it's finished so she can move on.

You might be able to see that Jane's reactive state – hope – keeps her in a miserable place. Her subconscious won't let her look at anybody else because it believes (a very simple bit of kit, is the subconscious) that they still share something. It might believe this for ages, in fact, because an odd thing about the subconscious is that it doesn't 'do' time. Time simply doesn't exist in that part of the psyche; there, something is or it is not. In Jane's case, her ex-boyfriend is still somewhere around as far as the subconscious is concerned – because she keeps him active in her mind – and so she has to sit and wait for him. Alice, though, has made the decision that it's over. Finished. The pain is short-lived as a result and she's able to move on.

Obviously, it's not always that easy. But when something is no longer, all the misery in the world won't change that fact. All that will happen is that the situation will stay the same *and* you feel awful. It doesn't matter what it is – your youth, a partner, your looks, your health... if it can't come back, it can't come back. It is what it is, and the task is to accept this is the case and move on. Surprisingly, perhaps, when the recognition is made and accepted that what has been lost cannot be recovered, the pain lessens dramatically and very soon stops altogether. It's that inner recognition, decision and acceptance that's so important.

One thing that is enormously important is where you have a problem with your physical self. Maybe you don't look the way you would like to look, or you think everybody looks better than you. Whatever, it means you're comparing yourself with somebody else, or with some ideal image you have in your mind. It might even be that you've made several changes to your appearance and yet you still feel the same... In these circumstances, it's highly likely that it's not truly what you look like that's causing the problem but the way you *feel* about yourself. Not only is this a *reactive* state but it means you're comparing how you *feel* with how others *look*. But how you think they look says nothing about how they feel, so it's not valid. It's like comparing a spoon with angry. It doesn't make sense because they are two entirely different concepts. So make a decision to stop all that and accept that when you feel better, you will look better. And that's a great truth!

Don't despair if you're now feeling that you can't do any of this – we've only just started and *all* you need to do at this stage is understand the idea. Just that understanding, coupled with the exercises you will be doing in each part of the programme, will be sufficient to produce the changes to your thoughts that will eventually set you free. In fact, it's fair to say that if you've understood what you were reading about the active and reactive states, and acceptance, necessary positive changes are already taking place without you even realising it!

Change

In many ways, change is easier to manage than acceptance, because the brain responds better to new possibilities than it does to old and unsatisfactory facts. Change can just as easily be active as destructively reactive. Reactive change includes the 'knee jerk' reaction or 'cutting off your nose to spite your face' – in other words, doing something purely for effect or to prove something to another, instead of seeking improvement. It's never a good idea, because it so frequently turns out to be change into something you *don't* want.

Active change is always involved with taking charge of your life in some way. The difficulty with this often lies in finding the energy to get started, since depression is extraordinarily weakening to both the mind and the body. This is where an *act of will* can be usefully employed. No matter how lethargic or depleted you feel, in the absence of genuine physical illness you *can* make a supreme effort to complete one task at a time. To begin, you need to think of a situation that you would like to change – and always remember, it must be *possible* for change to occur, even if it's difficult. Now you need to consider what options you have that *could* create that positive change. Here's an exercise that will help:

*Bring whatever problem you've decided to work on to mind and let it be there for a few minutes until the discomfort begins to fade a bit – it will always do so, since as mentioned before, the brain cannot maintain any stimulus indefinitely. **Want** it to fade and it will.*

*Then imagine somebody you know who is very resourceful – it can even be a film character if you like – finding a way to **start** to deal with the situation, in other words, what they would do to begin with. Follow it through in your mind until the problem is solved, **making it totally realistic,** then ask yourself if you could do what they did to **start** the process. It doesn't matter at this stage if you don't feel strong enough to complete the entire task. If the answer is 'no' then repeat the exercise, looking for a different **start** point and when you find one that 'works' for you, write it down (don't just commit it to memory – you must 'take action' on the idea to encourage your subconscious to give you more ideas, and writing it down counts as action.) Now decide on a time within the next two or three days – and set an exact time in your mind – that you will act upon what you've written down. And this is where the 'act of will' comes in: Know and understand that no matter what gets in your way or how you feel at the allotted time, **you will do that task!** No excuses. If your life depended on it, then you would do it. And when it's done, be pleased with yourself!*

Now, of course you could repeat the exercise every day and do a bit more of the task each time if you wanted to but the object of the work in this part of the programme is to get you started. It's a great confidence booster and you can come back to this exercise any time you wish.

Here's something to think about: *If there's something you don't like about yourself, change it; if you can't change it, then accept it… and if you have to accept it but you know it's something that's socially undesirable, control it with all your might.*

There are many, many thousands of people around the world who have to take that last bit of advice…

Continuing work

You can work through that 'Questionnaire One' list, taking each element in turn if you feel like it – some people do just that, grabbing the opportunity to at least make a start on sorting everything out. Or you can decide instead just to work at one or two elements, building your confidence and tackling the more difficult things later on, when you've discovered that you really are able to make profound and lasting changes in your life. It's your choice and as long as you make the decision yourself, you're taking charge of your life.

The surprise

The subtitle of this chapter was: *'Some questions and a surprise...'* Well, you've had the questions (though there are more to come) so we'd better get onto the surprise. This is all about an illustration which will show you how powerfully your posture and your speech pattern can affect your mood. Now don't get all alarmed – we're not about to embark on a *'shoulders back, chest out, step it out'* exercise but it does have a physical component to it. You have to stand up for this one. Read it through first so that you don't have to interrupt it once you've started and if you find it difficult; just do your best with it.

Stand with your feet apart, legs straight, arms thrown up into the air as if you are experiencing a moment of great joy, like winning several million pounds on the lottery, for instance. Now do your best to get the same expression of huge delight and joy on your face so that your whole being appears to be lit up with excitement – go on, it's only an act! Now, with your body and face holding the same expression say something like: "Oh God, I'm so depressed today," and make it sound as despairing as you can but without changing your facial expression or your body stance.

Do it now!

What did you discover? It's likely that you just couldn't complete the exercise as it's written because as soon as you started speaking, your face had to change and probably also your body posture. It's nearly impossible, even for accomplished actors, to take a body stance and facial expression of joy and maintain it while sounding as if they are in the depths of despair.

And that leads us nicely to the last little exercise of step one of this seven-step programme. This one is simple – all you need is a mirror. There is actually a choice of exercises here and you can do either or both, several times a day.

Yes, really!

Exercise 1: *Stand in front of the mirror and SMILE at yourself as broadly as you can, the same sort of smile you might give somebody if you want to make them feel really good. Smile up to your eyes, and mean it!*

You only need to do that for just a few seconds and experiments have shown that it actually does change body chemistry! This is probably because the physical brain recognises that somebody is smiling in your direction, which must mean you are valued. It's the smile that is the pattern being recognised and the fact that it's your own face doing the smiling is not important.

Exercise 2: *Stand in front of the mirror and 'high-five' yourself with a BIG smile and say something like: "You're the man!" or "Girl, you're amazing!" and really sound as if you mean it.*

It works for pretty much the same reasons as given above for the first exercise – but you really do need to act **extravagantly and enthusiastically**, even though it might feel totally fake... But don't be surprised if the smile lingers a little longer than you thought it might...

And that's it for the first step of the programme. You're on your way!

Building Anew

Creating sound foundations

We're going to be rebuilding the way you think about yourself, the way you work and the way you feel. Any building or rebuilding needs firm foundations if the work is to stand the test of time, of course, and the aim of this book is get you better *permanently.* The degree of 'betterness' is up to you, and that's great news because it means that you are in charge of your own recovery with the guidance of an expert!

We've already started laying the foundations, in step one, but before we can go any further, we need to make sure that all the materials we have to work with are ready and in exactly the condition we want. So step two takes a good look at the way you currently function and helps you make some adjustments where they are needed. Be warned though – this part of the programme might irritate you, make you angry, or even have you yelling at the pages in protest! But it will do something else as well... it will take you a little further along the road to getting better.

Chapter Three

An uncomfortable secret

As unlikely as it might seem to you right at this moment, it is entirely possible for you to get yourself free from this prison of depression. Thousands – millions – of others worldwide have escaped it before you. Now it's your turn. But first, be aware that this is not a nice, kind, sympathetic chapter. Sympathy does more for the giver than it does for the getter and never really made anybody feel much better, nor for very long. So instead, we will be investigating some of the uncomfortable secrets that lurk in the mind and psyche of almost everybody who experiences depression.

For many the first one is the most uncomfortable but be sure to think hard about it; if you can *honestly* say that this doesn't apply to you (and nobody will know one way or the other), that's excellent. It will make it even easier for you to get to where you want to be. On the other hand, if it's true but you deny it, you will be getting in your own way and stopping your own improvement... which, as daft as it sounds, might be exactly what you want to do.

This is secret number one, the most important one: *Many people suffering depression seek to avoid feeling better.*

Now, before you instantly dismiss the idea as unkind and ridiculous (which is a totally natural response) ask yourself how you tend to react if anybody offers an idea that is designed to make you feel better. Do you:

1. Try it whole-heartedly and check to see if you feel better?
2. Try it half-heartedly and check to see if you still feel depressed?
3. Thank them and say you'll try it even though you know you won't?

4. Tell them immediately that it wouldn't work for you?

If you answered number 1, then that's good (as long as it was honest!) and you can skip to the heading **'What's Going On?'** below, if you want to. The other answers show **resistance**, the biggest foe to the relief of depression, in ever increasing levels. We'll have a look at that situation – and no turning away from the truth here however uncomfortable it is if you *really* want to get better! Later, you'll see that there's no criticism being levelled in your direction, just a gradual move towards enlightenment that will carry you closer to the time when you can be free and *know* you're free.

If you answered '2': Why would you not give it a proper try and why check to see if you still feel depressed afterwards? It is a fact that you'll almost always discover what you look for and simply not see anything else – that's the way the brain works. If you were looking for red jackets in a shop, you wouldn't notice black trousers! So you can learn from this to always look for what you want.

If you answered '3': What would make you decide to not even give it a try? Perhaps you feel you couldn't be bothered or it was too much effort... which is a reaction the subconscious will give you. It's designed to make you give up before you've even started and, of course, it's enormously effective. But you do have to wonder what on earth is going on when you've turned down the opportunity to improve the way you feel...

If you answered '4': You really are falling over yourself to stay depressed! That might not make any sense at all – though it also makes no sense to say that something won't work without trying it first. You might be absolutely certain in your own mind that whatever is being suggested just won't work for you – and you'd be right. Not because of what it is, but because your subconscious knows you won't let it. Whatever was being suggested might very well turn out to be of no use... But that's not the point. The point is your subconscious was pretty determined that you shouldn't even give it a try. It rejected the notion out of hand and made sure you gave it not the slightest chance of working!

Arbut and Yerbut

There's another response which many people who know depression 'from the inside' might fall prey to, and that's to actually defend the 'ownership' of the depression. It's pretty much invisible to them though not to others. It's usually triggered when somebody tries to help by offering an idea that they know for sure has helped somebody else. The 'defending the ownership' goes like this (and this is where you find Arbut and Yerbut):

"Ah but (Arbut) I've had my depression longer than they had."
"Ah but I don't think you realise that wouldn't work for me because..."
"Ah but mine's a different sort of depression."
"Yeah but (Yerbut) I heard it doesn't last."
"Yeah but I heard somebody else tried that and it did nothing."
"Yeah but everybody knows depression is really difficult to fix."

Now, having got this far, here's another important question: Did you do the exercises in section one of this programme (Chapters One and Two)? If you didn't, then you have a decision to make. There are three choices:

1. Go back to the beginning and do the exercises before continuing. Just reading about them won't do anything.
2. Read the rest of the book and then throw it away (because once you've finished it you won't actually do anything more with it.)
3. Throw the book away now (then you won't waste any time with option 2)

This might all seem to be a bit of a tough stance that is upsetting in some way. But depression is tough. Living with it is tough... and when this programme is on the tough side it's because fixing it is tough. But it's *only* tough and you can do it. Anyway, you're still here, so hopefully you've completed the exercises in the first part of the programme and we can now crack on with getting you sorted out. Just as a 'belt and braces' statement though: there's a FAR higher chance of fantastic success if you do the exercises as they appear.

What's going on?

Okay, we've done some tough work so now we'll take things a bit easier and have a look at what on earth might be going on 'behind the scenes', in the depths of your subconscious. Even if you've answered every question with total honesty and come through them with flying colours, there will still be something to bring out into the open, where we can start to deal with it.

Time for the next uncomfortable secret now: *Many people derive some sort of benefit from 'their' depression.*

Now, you might be scoffing at that and deciding that the author hasn't got the first idea about what depression feels like (you'd be totally wrong) or that the idea of some sort of 'benefit' is patently ridiculous. Most people who experience depression feel like that – but that's a common part of the pattern. It saves having to look to see if there's an uncomfortable truth there somewhere. Well, if there *isn't* a truth, it won't hurt to properly explore the notion, so that you can then be justified in your dismissal of the whole idea. Or you can instead be pleased that while some people are trapped like that, you're not.

In the world of psychology, this process is well known and referred to as a **Hidden Agenda** or **Secondary Gain**. The processes are very similar and for our purposes here you can consider them to be the same. It means simply that the subconscious is using the depression to maintain a situation of some sort in which there is some perceived advantage. In fact, the advantage could be real, but the price is that you have to stay depressed. You might well not consciously realise what's happening just yet, or you might already have the germ of an understanding. It doesn't matter which, because we're going to investigate some of the more common aspects of the condition and it's likely that you will then begin to 'get it' if it applies to you. We'll begin with an obvious question: *What does depression actually do for you?* The answer might be any of the following:

- **It gets you attention:** It certainly does that but it's from people who view you as not very strong and just not able to cope with ordinary life. Some of them might even think of you as inferior.
- **It gets you off doing something:** But it **stops** you doing everything else!
- **It makes people feel sorry for you:** There's no real gain in this. Try to discover why you would want this situation and work at letting it go.
- **People do things for you:** Although they won't usually tell you, it's quite often because they feel under some sort of obligation.
- **People go out of their way to look after you:** This might make you feel loved... but it's not love in the positive sense. It might not even be love at all but something far less comfortable.
- **It provides an excuse for failing:** Get rid of it and be a success instead!
- **It sets you apart from the 'common crowd':** Yes, it makes you 'special'. But it's far better to be impressively special instead of depressively so.

It might be the case that none of the above seem to 'fit' the way you feel though if something else has come to mind do be certain to explore it! You haven't got to do anything with it just yet, except acknowledge that it's there and that you really would like to be able to let it go, albeit reluctantly. That's not easy, of course, especially since the depression has almost certainly become part of your identity... people know you as a depressed person. They reinforce the situation every time they see you or ask you how you are. Your answers reinforce the situation still further... so in the words of a very old song, Something's Gotta Give!

The deadly embrace

This is the original 'Catch 22' situation. *You can't function like other people because of 'your' depression... and you already know it's no good trying to deal with 'your' depression because you can't function like other people can.* That's the Deadly Embrace in action and you can probably see the flaw in the circular argument, now it's put in front of you. And yet many people continue to labour under that sort of misapprehension without realising how limiting – and how fake – it is. This is why it's so important to closely examine the way depression affects your life, so here's a simple exercise that will explore the possibility of a Deadly Embrace getting in the way if you start getting better. This one is best done with your eyes closed, so read the passage in italics through to the end and be sure you understand what you need to do. It's a good idea to make sure you won't be disturbed for around thirty minutes or so, so put your phone into silent mode and ask anybody else in the building not to interrupt you.

*With your eyes closed to avoid other distracting inputs; let your mind drift through the events of any recent day. It can be yesterday or the day before, or any other day but the important thing is that you must be able to recall it in good detail. Run through it from morning to evening a couple of times. Now remember the individual, either real or imagined, who has plenty of resource (the one you thought of in the 'mirror exercise' in **step one**.) When you* *have them in your mind, go through that typical day again but this time as if you had exactly the same resources as that person. Make sure you avoid resisting what you would do differently – it's only a 'thought experiment' and nobody is saying you have to start being that person. It's time for honesty though! Let yourself notice what would be different and ask yourself if there is any reason on earth why you would not be able to behave like that if you didn't have the depression. Maybe it's just something you wouldn't **want** to do – and that's okay. Decide that you won't ever do that and to hell with what anybody else thinks. Explore everything that would work differently from the way it does now and ask yourself how it would feel if you could already do it, ignoring any notion that the depression would somehow mess everything up. You wouldn't even **have** the depression if that version of you was real, would you? And if it's possible for **somebody** to do it (and it must be because you thought of it) then why not you, once the depression has been dealt with?*

Now, if you feel even the tiniest bit uplifted after you've completed that exercise, then you're doing just fine and there's nothing else to work at for the moment. If you find yourself resisting the notion, though, then it probably has something to do with Arbut and Yerbut and secondary gain. And here's another 'secret' which might or might not apply to you:

Many people with depression really don't want other people to believe they might be getting better.

If that's truly not you, excellent! If it does describe you, though, ask yourself why you work like that – it's probably for one of those reasons listed earlier. Here they are again:

- **It gets you attention**
- **It gets you off doing something**
- **It makes people feel sorry for you**
- **People do things for you**

- **People go out of their way to look after you**
- **It provides an excuse for failing**
- **It sets you apart from the 'common crowd'**

More questions now: *(1) Does any of it make you feel good? (2) If it does, why are you still depressed? (3) Will you carry on with this thing forever? (4) Would you have more fun in life if you joined in instead of being the one who can't do things?*

Answer them as accurately as you can and then you can make a decision based on your answers. If you answered 'yes' to questions 1 and 3 then you probably couldn't actually answer question 2 at all. But what it means is that as daft as it might sound, you are actually *happy* with 'your' depression. In that case, you won't make any real efforts to fix it and this book has nothing for you – you've discovered you are exactly where and how you want to be, so just enjoy it. Privately, of course!

If you answered 'Yes' to question 4 though, you really are on the right path to getting better! And all you have to do is to continue reading and complete the questionnaires and exercises as they appear.

Now, if you feel that nothing much is changing, don't worry, because it simply means we have not yet happened across the reason for the depression that *you* experience. But there's a long way to go yet and a lot of ground to cover, so read on and allow yourself to find understandings and enlightenment where you can. Some people have a 'light bulb' moment, while others have a more gradual change. But one thing's for sure. *It's very nearly impossible to complete this seven-step programme without creating* **some** *positive change.*

Questionnaire Two

Well, we did say there would be a lot of questions... you can think of them as quizzes if you like, because that often makes them seem more interesting! Just as well, too, because just like busses there'll be another one along in a minute... You might already have noticed, though, that all these questions are helping you to get inside your own head. They help you to understand where the depression is coming from and that, along with the exercises, 'thought experiments' and other information you are reading about will provide the stepping stones to the new you. Look forward to it!

So, here's the questionnaire, which is all about how often you feel certain reactions (the reasons are not important here) and you should score each of the following as close to the truth as possible. Score 1 if your answer is 'Never' or 'Rarely', 2 for 'Sometimes' and 3 for 'Often'.

Reactions score

- Irritated
- Jealous
- Pessimistic
- Bored
- Frustrated
- Cheated
- Sad
- Lonely
- Put upon

If your total score is 9 (the lowest possible) then you might need to have another think! Very few people indeed could say 'never' to every single question in that list, and the same is likely to be the case if you have scored 27 (the maximum). Think about this for a moment... it's not likely that you are *never* 'Jealous' or *never* feel 'Cheated'; and in the same way, you're not likely to *often* feel bored and *often* feel irritated! Answering everything with a score of 2 isn't much better either, since there are very few people (even depressed ones) who feel *all* of those 'Sometimes'. Answers like these usually indicate either the wish to complete the questionnaire without having to make too much effort, or the presence of the Hidden Agenda against getting better that was mentioned earlier. So if you've answered with the same score to every reaction go through the list again and think about it in more detail – and if it has revealed the possibility of a Hidden Agenda, see if you can root it out and deal with it... Or at least understand it.

Your answers to this particular questionnaire say far more than you might realise at this stage and you need them to be accurate, because you'll soon see how they contribute to your freedom.

Okay, one more 'quiz' for this chapter.

Questionnaire Three

First, think about how you feel on a day-to-basis in general. Depressed, of course, but it's usually not at its worst most of the time. When you have that in your mind, classify that as having a score of '0'. Now, choose which one of the following 'life situations' would make it worse – and be sure to choose the worst:

1. *Criticism/dismissal by others*
2. *Making mistakes*
3. *Not being in control*
4. *Being called dull or drab*
5. *Having no sex*
6. *Being ridiculed*
7. *Having no friends*
8. *Being let down by others*
9. *Being misunderstood*

Now decide how **much** worse what you have chosen would make you feel, scoring it between 1 and 50 and making a note of the answer.

Now we're going to do the exact opposite, so this time choose from the following situations the one that would actually lift your mood and make you feel better – and again choose the one that would affect you most:

1. *Finally putting somebody in their place*
2. *Proving you were right*
3. *Catching a liar out*
4. *Winning a talent competition*
5. *Impressing others*
6. *Becoming famous*
7. *Being looked after by others*
8. *Discovering somebody values you as a friend*
9. *Being told you are loved*

Again, decide just how **much** better whatever you have chosen would make you feel and score it between 1 and 50.

Now, adding the two numbers together represents the amount of energy (as a percentage of the total energy in your mind) you have available to make changes in your life. This might not make a lot of sense until you can recognise that the extremes that you can *feel* in your mind are the same as the extremes of what you can *create* in your mind. If you still don't quite 'get' that, just trust and accept that, although it might seem odd, it's the capacity for change that's important. Of course, we're going to get the change to be for the better, but for the moment just accept that the higher the number the easier it will be for you to create that change. You might want to have another look at the questionnaire now to make sure you've chosen the very best thing as well as the very worst. Never mind about what's nice or fair – choose what works for *YOU*!

Consistency

There's just one last thing to do for this chapter and that is to check for the consistency of your responses. This is actually easy to do using the answers you've given to the last two questionnaires. Add together the scores for the first three questions on **Questionnaire Two**, then for the next three, and finally for the last three, so you now have three numbers. Write them down, because you'll need them again later. To help you remember them, call them **Q2/1**, **Q2/2** and **Q2/3**. Note the highest one of those and if there isn't a highest one, or there are two highest or all three that are the same, choose the first one. For instance, if **Q2/1** was the same as **Q2/2** or **Q2/3**, you would choose **Q2/1**.

Next, look at your answers for 'What makes it worse'. If your answer is in the first three of the list, call it **W1**, **W2** if it's in the second group of three, and **W3** if it's in the last group. Finally look to see in which group is your answer to 'What makes it better'. If it's in the first three, name it **B1**, in the second group it's **B2** and, of course, in the third group, it's **B3**

Now, if you are consistent, then you will have one of these patterns:

- **Q2/1**, **W1**, **B1**
- **Q2/2**, **W2**, **B2**
- **Q2/3**, **W3**, **B3**

An extreme of inconsistency would be something like: **Q2/1**, **W2**, **B3** – but don't worry if you discover that's the way you are! In fact, it accounts for the depression you are experiencing and you will definitely benefit greatly from this programme. There's a section especially for you on dealing with inconsistency which will help even more.

Of course, if you are already pretty consistent, that stability is going to help you greatly, as long as you can avoid self-sabotage and pessimism... which is what the next chapter is all about!

Chapter Four

Auto-pessimism and self-sabotage

It is a fact that optimistic people have more fun in life – and they live longer too. There's no mystery here. The pessimist sees only the downside of everything, no matter how good others might perceive it to be. The optimist perceives the possibility of something rewarding in even the darkest moment and because of this has more to live for... And it is a well-established fact that those who have a good reason to stay alive are likely to do so for longer, as well as more happily.

Optimism and pessimism are both habits (though the tendency towards either appears to be partly inherited) and like all habits, they can be acquired by repetition. In other words, if you have a tendency towards pessimism, you can *learn* to be optimistic by determinedly practising seeing the best in things – it's always there. The two approaches colour what you see and what you think and feel, as the following story shows. It's actually a joke but it highlights the difference that habitual thinking can make:

Alice and Bob have twin sons, one of whom is a pessimist and the other an outrageous optimist. One Christmas, they decide they will help each recognise that things don't always turn out the way you think, since they consider this to be an important lesson in life. So they buy the pessimist, who has been grumbling depressively that he hates Christmas because it's always boring, everything he could ever want. For the optimist, who has been hyperactively looking forward to Christmas and the wonderful things it might bring, they buy a pile of horse manure.

Come Christmas morning, they make their way to the first one, who is sitting dejectedly amongst all sorts of 'goodies' complaining that there are no batteries for the laser pointer, the laptop probably won't work, the mobile phone will almost certainly get stolen, he's already got the books, the remote controlled car doesn't reverse, and he doesn't understand what he's supposed to do with a science kit...

The parents sigh in disappointment and go to see their other son, who, when they find him, is in the middle of the pile of manure, busily flinging it about left and right and all over the place. "Stop, stop!" the parents exclaim. "What on earth are you doing?" Their son looks up, his face alight with excitement. "With all this s**t about," he says breathlessly, "There's got to be a horse in here somewhere!"

It's doubtful that the optimistic brother would have found a horse but he was still happier than his twin, even then. To seek something with enthusiastic optimism, yet still not find what you're looking for, is far better than pessimistic assumption. And if you're going to search anyway, *be careful what you look for in case you find it!*

Here are four important facts:

1. If you keep looking for 'bad stuff' you'll eventually find it.
2. If you keep looking for 'good stuff' you'll eventually find it.
3. While you're looking for one, you won't even *see* the other.
4. As soon as you find what you're looking for, you stop searching – so you won't ever notice the other most of the time.

If you suffer from auto-pessimism – that is you tend to automatically look for what's wrong with an idea or concept, what the 'catch' is, without even thinking about it – it can be quite difficult to learn the habit of optimism. In fact, you might not even want to... But it can be nearly impossible to banish depression while maintaining a fully active state of auto-pessimism!

Now, you might be rebelling against the idea of being optimistic, or it could seem to be a mountainous task, just too difficult to contemplate. Perhaps you feel as if you might somehow be at risk if you don't keep an eye out for what might go wrong. Those responses are common 'trademarks' of depression (although it's not fair to say that everybody who thinks like that is depressed.) But it's worth two powerful recognitions:

1. Becoming an optimist doesn't actually take any effort – it's just a thought process that you can easily adopt; the next time you are feeling depressed about the possible outcome of a situation, *write down* what you would prefer to happen instead. It doesn't matter if you don't believe it, because the exercise is only meant to loosen the automatic negative response – it will start to create doubt about the reality of your doubt!

2. If you're worried that you might be at risk somehow, becoming an optimist doesn't make you blind! An optimist will still see all the pitfalls just as clearly but instead of fretting about them in despairing mode, they will immediately begin to seek – and find – solutions. The optimist *knows* there's an answer and looks for it, while the pessimist fears there isn't and dwells upon the awfulness. Can you tell which one is active and which is *re*active?

Self-sabotage

Sometimes, the subconscious plays invisible tricks on the depressed mind, possibly to avoid the perceived risk of moving away from the depressed state, which is familiar and predictable, to a state that's unfamiliar and therefore unpredictable. You can test for this very easily by spending just a few minutes thinking about what you would do if you were not depressed. *Really* think about it, in fine detail. Not just: *"I'd change my job,"* for example, but how you would do that, what you would do and how would you go about it. If your instant response was: *"I don't know,"* then it's highly likely that your subconscious is holding you locked into one of two enormously clever bits of self-sabotage!

The first one is to ensure that you spend a lot of time thinking about past failures, past disappointments, missed opportunities, and so on... *and if you're busy thinking about the past, which you cannot change, you are ignoring the future, which you **can** change!* And think carefully about this next bit... While you were busy thinking about the past yesterday, tomorrow was sneaking up on you to soon become another yesterday. In other words while you were thinking about the past, the future was already whizzing past you!

The second subconscious trick is no less destructive. In this situation, you spend a lot of your time dreading tomorrow or the next day for fear that you might get worse or that some disaster will befall you. So in this version of the trickery, the subconscious has you locked into the notion that there is definitely more misery in front of you, when the truth is that the future hasn't happened yet and is there for you to do with what you want. Here's another thing to think carefully about: today is the tomorrow you were worrying about yesterday and now all you have to worry about is tomorrow.

Of course it might be the case that you're now saying something along the lines of: *"That's all very well, but I don't fit into either of those categories, so now what?"* Well, if that's the case, then your category is the best one, the one where you're living in the actual moment. You're not dwelling on the past or second-guessing what lies in front of you; you're already in the best place to start making changes for the future – the moment of *now*. Whatever has gone before, you are ready to start making changes, and we're going to start on that process very shortly.

Now, if you're in one of the first two categories – stuck in the past or holding back from the future – we have to show you how to get to that moment of *now* that's so important. At first, you might not be able to stay in it for very long at a time (because old habits die hard!) and you'll need to practise it a bit until you can go there whenever you decide to. Only then can you begin your journey out of the dark and grey world of depression to that place most people call 'normal'. To get into the moment of *now*, you're going to perform a simple exercise that seems not at all remarkable at first but it will pave the way for some of the more advanced things you will learn later on. It has a side effect that *is* quite remarkable though, in that it will suspend your misery about the past or your horror of the future (or both of those) leaving you feeling neutral. Ordinary. Nothing special like 'happy' (that's an imposter anyway, since it's a reaction, not an emotional state) or 'light-hearted', or any other devil-may-care situation you can think of. Just ordinary. It can feel odd at first until you get used to it, when you recognise that it's rather nice, just being, without fretting about how useless you feel.

The exercise doesn't need any special skill or preparation; whenever you feel ready is exactly the right time to do it and we'll assume that, since you're here, you're in the right frame of mind to have a go at it now. To begin, find a comfortable place to sit and just relax as much as you can for a moment or two. Good. Now just concentrate on your breathing. Count up to five while you breathe in and up to eight as you breathe out, counting at the same speed. Listen to the sound your breath makes and how it feels. It might sound different when you breathe out from when you breathe in. It might *feel* different when you breathe out from when you breathe in. If you could give those feelings and sounds a colour, what would they be? Would they be different tones of the same colour or would they be different colours altogether? Or is there not really any colour at all? How does your body feel as you notice your breathing? Do you feel less tense or more tense? (It doesn't actually matter which at this stage, as long as you can notice it.) Investigate each part of the whole process in detail until you are so familiar with it that you can identify each part in your mind in some way:

- The way a breath in for a count of five feels
- If there is a colour associated with it
- The way a breath out for a count of eight feels
- If there's a colour associated with it
- How your body feels overall

Now, while you were doing all that you were actually in the moment of *now*. You couldn't *not* be, since you were having to think about several things in succession and we can only think of one thing at a time, so while your mind was busy with the exercise, you weren't pondering on the past or feeling anxious about the future. Because you were busy thinking of the exercise, you wouldn't have noticed that you weren't thinking about your usual 'stuff'. You might even have discovered a rather odd feeling of quietness, as if your mind had stopped doing what it usually does for a moment or two... And if you didn't, then try it now. Think about the moment of *now* and concentrate on it. Really concentrate on it so that you're thinking about nothing else.

That's a very simple version of something called *mindfulness meditation* which is an excellent way of 'getting away from yourself' for a little while; it allows your mind to become quiet and during that quietness, there's no emotion. That means no misery, no depression, just a sense of quietness. There's a bonus, too, in that many researchers have indicated that it is in itself an aid to beating depression.

Now we're going to move on to a couple of exercises that will prepare your mind for change – and will almost certainly start the process of creating it.

But reversal

This is easy to do and understand but can be difficult to maintain because of sheer force of habit, so you'll need to practise it. Most people use the word 'but' in a completely negative way that stops them from achieving anything or making any improvement in their lives. And yet, with just a tiny bit of thought, it can be turned into one of the most magical words you will ever have encountered! Consider the following two statements:

- *"I'd like to do more with my life but this depression makes it difficult."*
- *"This depression makes it difficult but I'm going to do more with my life."*

You can probably already see why this exercise is so important. The first statement actively *stops* any ideas of how to get on with life, whereas the second one *encourages* them. Okay, it might only prompt the question: *"How?"* at this stage, but searching for an answer is a whole lot better than believing there isn't one, don't you think? And it's an interesting fact that if a question is posed to your subconscious, it begins immediately to search for a solution and it will continue to do that until it finds one.

Like most people, you've probably encountered the situation where you're struggling to remember somebody's name or some other thing that you're sure you know but just can't bring to the front of your mind. Again like most people, you've probably eventually given up on the idea as something else attracted your attention... And then, when you're not even thinking about it, maybe even a day or two later, it's suddenly there in your mind! You might have wondered how on earth that happens, and the answer is quite simple – you asked a question of your subconscious and it obediently searched for the answer. That's what it does and it can't *not*, because that's the way our brain's 'wired'.

So you can now begin to see why that 'but reversal' trick is so powerful – it triggers the subconscious to begin the search for an answer!

Nothing magical happens. Well, not that you'd notice as magical, anyway. But an idea will just suddenly be there in your mind, as long as you truly want it (and if you don't, then you're back to some of the 'resistance stuff' you've read about earlier.) And the important thing then, as has been mentioned before, is to take some kind of action – even just writing it down will do. Then, because you've actually *done something* with what it found, that obliging subconscious will begin to present you with a few more ideas, too.

So, whenever you find yourself saying 'but' (remember 'Arbut' and 'Yerbut'?) check to see if you have the positive statement *after* the 'but', exactly where it should be. Then stand by for the ideas to start arriving. It doesn't matter if you don't do anything with them at this stage, other than make a note of them, or even record them into your mobile phone or digital recorder – as long as you perform some sort of 'motor action', you are feeding the subconscious exactly what it needs, which is a positive response to what it produces. It's entirely possible that a lot of the ideas will not be valid for some reason or another – the subconscious is not very selective – but amongst them will be the occasional 'gem'. We'll come back to that process later on, but now we're going to move on to the next exercise.

The virtual world

This might lift your mood for a while but it's really designed mainly to get you thinking in a constructive manner, instead of a destructive one. Essentially, it's building on what you've already read, and the work you have already done, to help create the foundations of your new life. You'll need to find some time when you won't be disturbed, so find a private place and switch off your mobile (or put it on silent) and if there's anybody else in the building make it clear that they're to leave you alone for thirty minutes or so. You don't want interruptions here if they can be avoided. You'll need to do the exercise with your eyes closed if you're to get the best out of it, so do read through to the end of it before your start – and while you're reading it through, you can form the ideas in your mind that you'll be using.

To begin, settle yourself down comfortably, close your eyes, and do the 'breathing thing' to find the 'moment of now'. If you are able, you might prefer to just move into that quiet place where you're not really thinking of anything at all except the moment. When you've found that special quietness, choose any aspect of your life – where you live, relationships with others, personal confidence, energy levels, anything – and let yourself imagine exactly how you would like it to be. Make it vivid and energetic yet sensible and possible; in other words, be certain that it's something that *could* happen and do watch out for the misplaced 'but'! You haven't got to actually try to do whatever it is, only think about it, and you can, and should, make it as liberating as you are able. Don't worry about what others might think, because they don't know that you're doing this and anyway, you're working at changing *your* life, not theirs. See it like a short video clip, maybe just a minute or two, that keeps looping round and round, and every time it loops it becomes brighter and more realistic and maybe more detailed. Keep on playing the loop in your mind until it becomes so familiar that you could write it down in detail if you chose to. It's when you get to that point that it's the time to stop. Then give yourself a few seconds before opening your eyes.

You might want to take a short break before moving on to the next section where we're going to investigate a situation that's extraordinarily familiar where depression lurks. On the other hand, if you're feeling energised after that last exercise, this might be a good time to press on!

Anger

Most people with depression don't feel anger... they feel depressed instead. Many therapists believe that depression is frequently 'anger turned inwards' and though the idea is not always borne out by the facts, it is more often right than wrong. But it's an unusual sort of anger, in that it's directed at two people and if the argument is correct in your case we already know who one of those people is... It's **YOU!**

Now, you might want to argue about that and you might even be angry about it but if so, there's a very high chance that it *is* true for you even if you're feeling a bit indignant about the idea right now. In fact, *especially* if you're feeling a bit indignant about the idea right now. If you're not, well, maybe it doesn't apply in your case... but it still might. Either way, let yourself wonder, just for a moment or two, about who the other person could possibly be. It could be just about anybody you know, though it's likely to be somebody with whom there has been some sort of important relationship rather than a casual acquaintance. It can be somebody who has been dismissive of you when you looked up to them; it can be a parent, sibling, or other relative; it can be somebody who has accused you unjustly of something, or somebody who has somehow caused others to look at you in a poor light, for instance. It could even be the case that whoever it is did nothing at all other than just arrive and somehow displace you in some way. (A younger sibling isn't *necessarily* loved – they might inspire jealousy instead.)

If the anger concept is relevant in your case, you'll recognise it when you think of the right person – and by the way, the anger at *yourself* is usually for one of three reasons:

- You weren't able to address the situation, or were not listened to, and therefore see yourself as of little consequence
- You believe that you shouldn't have such feelings and are therefore a 'bad' person

- A combination of both the above

A case study

The third point, above, is quite common and a snippet or two from a real case can help you to understand how it works:

John, an only child whose father had left before he was born, was brought up in his early years by his mother. She remarried when he was six years old and it wasn't long before a half-sister, Mary, arrived. His mother and stepfather doted on their child and she was constantly praised for minor achievements, while John's efforts either passed unnoticed or were dismissed. Of course, he was not able to remonstrate with this situation and also believed – because he was told so – that he was a thoroughly unpleasant child because he was critical of Mary. He gradually withdrew into himself and became insular, not forming relationships very easily and certainly not able to maintain those that he did manage to get into. By his late teens, he was depressed and anxious, but this was also dismissed as being 'creepy'.

It was only many years later, in therapy, that he revisited the frustration and anger at his mother for remarrying; at his step-father for coming between him and his mother, and his later dismissiveness; his half-sister for being born; and himself for having proved the fact that he was unpleasant and of no consequence. Only now, as an adult, he could articulate it and recognise the areas where it was justified and so was able to let go of it – and with it went the depression that had beset him for years.

Through therapy, John was able to recognise that the crux of his problems was that his mother had remarried. He was easily able to see that this was not especially remarkable and that though what followed may have been unfair, it was another fairly unremarkable set of circumstances. He soon realised that he could fret forever about it all, or he could decide to leave it in the past, where it belonged, and just get on with his life.

The thing that *was* remarkable was that John had had no recognition of the anger that was still bubbling away in the depths of his mind – his subconscious created a state of depression instead. Depression is often a protection from more uncomfortable feelings, especially those that we feel unable to confront. So if you've 'unearthed' something uncomfortable in this chapter, recognise and accept that no matter what, you cannot undo the situation. Leave it back there in the past, as John did, and begin to move forward.

In the next stage of this programme, we're going to help you shake yourself free from another one of those tricks the subconscious mind plays...

A Change of View

I can see clearly... not

One of the most difficult things for the person with depression is to see clearly. Of course, you can look around you and see your surroundings. You can look down at yourself and see what you're wearing... or not. You can even look at the television, a book, a newspaper, or the pile of washing-up in the kitchen – but everything you look at is coloured by some very odd processes in the physical brain. You won't actually be aware of those, only the end result, which is the way they leave you feeling. And if anybody ever tells you to 'pull yourself together', you can point out that not one of us is able to control the way we feel, only what we do with those feelings.

You might want to argue with the last part of that statement, feeling that you have no ability to control the way you behave. But if you've ever changed your mind about something (and all of us have, of course) then that was controlling what you did with what you first felt, though there is much more to that than meets the eye, as you will see when we get to the last part of this programme.

Anyway, we're going to have a look now at some of those things that get in the way of clear vision, and how you might begin to see through them.

Chapter Five

The chaos of catastrophisation

Everybody does it sometimes but the individual who suffers depression is the most skilled and inventive at it. Catastrophisation. You'll recognise the sort of thing:

> *A brown window envelope from Inland Revenue drops onto your doormat with the post and you realise straight away that you must have forgotten to pay the bill... and you know how difficult they are. You'll probably get called down to their offices for an interview and you're bound to make such a mess of it that they'll think you're up to no good and want to investigate you further, and once they start on you they never stop until they find something. They'll probably think you've deliberately withheld information and tried to defraud them, so you're bound to end up in prison, which means your partner will leave you and you'll lose your house. And if that wasn't bad enough, because you've now got a criminal record you'll never be able to get a mortgage or maybe even be able to rent anywhere... you could even end up on the streets like so many others you've heard of...*

Okay, so that's a bit exaggerated but it's odds on that you've done something like it, even if not so extreme. Catastrophising, in case you needed more clarification, is the involuntary act of creating the worst possible outcome of a scenario in your mind and then behaving and feeling as if were true, with no further questions or consideration.

You might have noticed that it says 'involuntary' and now be wondering how on earth you can stop it. Well, it's only involuntary until you're alerted to how pointless and also how inaccurate it always is. After that, you can choose whether to indulge yourself with it or not. Some people, of a specific personality type that you'll be reading about in the next chapter, actually take a kind of perverse enjoyment in it... that is, until it starts to look as if they might have been accurate!

Usually, it doesn't take the form of a continuous stream of thoughts like those shown at the beginning of this chapter, not to start with, anyway. It's more just a feeling of doom that descends with the first event – in this case, the brown window envelope from the Inland Revenue landing on the doormat. And then the subconscious does a strange thing. It immediately starts to construct a scenario to justify that feeling of doom and so that nobody could argue with it, the worst-case scenario possible will start to appear in the conscious mind over a period of a few minutes or hours. But there's a flaw to this entire concept and that is that *all you know is all you know!* All you know is that you've received the envelope. It might contain nothing more threatening than information about how to pay your next bill when it's due; advice of a new tax code; a reminder that you have to complete your self-assessment forms; or even a tax rebate!

Now, a momentary anxiety on situations that *could* be threatening is pretty normal as a result of the evolution of our species – more about that shortly – but catastrophising isn't. It's learned in some way. And it can be *un*learned as long as you are able to remind yourself of that fact that *all you know is all you know.* To defeat it, you need a 'trigger' to help you remember that and create a much better response; a catchphrase, if you like, an automatic thing for you to say or think when confronted with something that *might* be 'a bit awkward'. You probably already have one of those actually – most people have. It's usually something like: *"Oh God..."* or: *"Now what?"*

Well, all you need to do is to replace it with another saying that will soon become automatic if you practise using it. A good one is something that people used to say quite frequently when there was something that they thought might need attention:

"Wait a minute!" Imagine that being said brightly in the sort of clipped accent you might hear in old films from the 1930s. Now, there's far more to that than you might at first realise. Not only will it stop the instant catastrophisation, but if it's followed with: *"What's this all about?"* it encourages an **active** response rather than a **reactive** one. You might remember reading about that in Chapter Two, with 'Jane and Alice':

> **Jane:** *"Oh no! This is disastrous! Why on earth does this sort of thing always happen to me? God knows how I'm supposed to get anywhere..."*

> **Alice:** *"Oops! That wasn't supposed to happen! Okay, there's got to be a good way for me to deal with this..."*

Here, you can clearly see the beginning of catastrophisation in Jane's response and given time, she would sink deeper into a pit of despair. Alice, on the other hand, has got her subconscious looking for an answer... and, as you now know, once you've asked a question of your subconscious it will begin to search for a solution.

Those expressions *"Wait a minute!"* and *"What's this all about?"* are, of course, quaintly old-fashioned – but that makes them easy to remember as long as you hear them in your 'mind's ear' being spoken in an old-fashioned style. Practise using them whenever something uncomfortable happens and it will soon become habit. It doesn't matter one jot if your first reaction – the feeling of doom – is the same as it always was, because *"Wait a minute!"* will stop that process in its tracks. And *"What's this all about?"* prepares your subconscious to start searching for a solution to whatever it *is* about.

Here are some examples of 'threat' scenarios that can trigger negative reactions; practise your best 1930s voice and allow yourself to find possible answers that are definitely not disastrous:

- Your partner says: *"We have to talk..."*
- Your boss says he needs to see you in his office *immediately.*
- A policeman stops you in the street with: *"One moment please."*
- A letter arrives with a lawyer's postmark on the envelope.
- The telephone rings in the middle of the night.

Expect to need to practise using your new response for a while before it becomes automatic, but be sure to use them every time you feel 'challenged', even it feels totally fake. That subconscious of yours will eventually get the idea of replacing the old 'unhelpful thought' with the new 'helpful' one. You can choose different things to say if you prefer, but do make sure they are specific enough for you to remember when you need them.

As a matter of interest, there is a distinct 'upside' to all this – if you are in the habit of catastrophising, it means you have a powerfully active imagination. Harness that power in a positive manner and you have one of the best tools available for beating the hell out of depression!

The unnaturalness of positive thinking

Many people will tell you that you must learn to always think positively if you're to have a chance of defeating depression. But it's actually completely 'normal' to feel a surge of something that's far from positive when an event that *could* indicate a problem occurs and you can blame that on *Australopithecus Africanus!* A. Africanus lived a couple of million years ago and was more ape than human. They were one of the earliest forms of hominims and would only have survived because of a genetic disposition that has been handed down through generations of our ancient ancestors, eventually finding its way into *homo sapiens sapiens* – that's us. That genetic disposition is the tendency to look for what might go wrong, in order to spot the pit before falling into it... and a dose of anxiety is an excellent warning signal that you need to *do* something to avoid trouble.

Those with the highest tendency to spot it were the most likely to survive, while those without it were the most likely to perish, and nature being what it is, it was only a matter of time before it was a natural process in every individual. And there lies a Very Important Clue as to why the modern idea that we must always think positively all the time just cannot work all the time – you were born with inherited instincts that worked against it! The problems our ancestors faced, though, weren't tax bills – they were threats to life and they knew they had to *do* something. Not only that, but their action would have to be pretty immediate, just as the threats were. There was no time to think, no time to catastrophise, only time for action.

Now, threats are usually slower-paced these day. Most of the time, anyway. If you're crossing the road and there's the sudden blare of a car horn, you will do exactly what your ancestors did when *they* found trouble heading their way – you'll get quickly out of the way without catastrophising over how you could end up in hospital, lose your job, be out on the streets, and so on. More often than not, though, there *is* time to think, deliberate and catastrophise... So, how can we stop this from happening? Easy! By making sure you take instant action the very moment a threat scenario appears on the scene:

"Wait a minute! What's this all about?"

That response does all sorts of useful things. It satisfies your subconscious that you have taken action and that you are looking for a solution to the problem. No need to create imaginary scenarios to justify the anxiety or sense of doom. In fact, you probably won't get a sense of doom because you've already diverted the subconscious processes to something far more important (it will only work on one idea at a time) and that is to discover everything about what's happened in order to take the best course of action.

Okay, so we now know that 'positive thinking' is not a natural thing to do at all... But that doesn't mean that it's pointless or unnecessary. What you need to do is learn the trick the most successful people do almost without knowing it: find out exactly what the difficulty is, *then* start thinking positively about it. It's a fact that for any problem there is always more than one solution and all you have to do is find it. If you're prone to catastrophisation, then you already have everything you need to find the answer... a powerful imagination. Let your mind run over every possibility you can think of – the good ones as well as the less useful – all the time knowing there's definitely a solution to the problem waiting to be found.

What you dream up might not be ideal, and it might not be exactly what you wanted... but it definitely beats catastrophising! More importantly, perhaps, that subconscious knowledge that you *will* always seek a solution to life's difficulties chips away at the tendency towards depression.

Guilt, shame and embarrassment

Guilt, Shame and Embarrassment are like evil cousins! They achieve little that is positive, much that is destructive, and it's even a puzzle to some why we have the capacity to experience them in the first place. You can't suffer one without at least one of the other two, and it's more likely that you'll find all three at once. Most people who experience depression tend to suffer higher than usual levels of these responses – or more accurately, they experience them for longer. This is because depression is a peculiarly self-obsessed condition; if the individual who suffers it *does* think about anybody else for a while, it's usually concerned with what that other person thinks about *them*. There is no criticism in this – it's just the way that depression works. It's certainly not a voluntary process, nor can it be voluntarily suspended, and as a result there's more often than not an inflated idea of the importance of the 'downsides' of self, and so it is that they are examined over and again *ad infinitum*. You can probably see how that eventually becomes part of the catastrophisation process.

If this all seems horribly familiar to you, the first thing to take on trust is that no matter what *you* think of whatever event or series of events is creating such powerful feelings, others will think about it only momentarily. If at all. Because the human animal is essentially egocentric, we quickly get bored when we think about others for very long. Even the nastiest public scandals quickly become yesterday's news and the only time anybody thinks about them after the initial flurry of scandalised interest is if they are revisited in the media for any reason. So anything you've been up to in the past has probably been long-forgotten by others. Unless you keep on reminding them, of course... Or maybe the problem is that you have a secret you consider to be disgusting, and you fear it coming out one day. Well, if anybody else knows about it, there's always that chance but, again, it would seem far less important to others than it does to you and they'd soon forget all about it.

The other possibility is that you have a 'dark secret' that only you know about, but that still causes you problems if it comes to mind. If that's the case, it can be dealt with quite easily and here's how: First, do the 'breathing thing' to find the 'moment of now', then in your imagination, turn the secret into a still photograph and make it black and white. Once that's done, conjure up a safe with a combination lock in your mind, place the photograph inside it and slam the door shut, hearing it 'clunk' in your mind's ear. Before you spin the lock (this bit is Very Important) make a note of the combination number you choose, just as if it were a real safe. Write it down if you feel the need to. Now, in your mind, spin the combination lock several times so nobody could ever open it without knowing the number.

It doesn't sound like very much but from now on, if that secret ever starts to bother you, all you need to do is to think of the combination number in your mind and any uncomfortable feelings will immediately begin to fade.

But let's have a close look at this whole process. Whatever the cause, it's back there in the past and cannot be altered. Assuming that it's not something illegal or immoral that you're still doing (which would actually be beyond the scope of this book) then you can afford to let it fade into the mists of time. If you doubt this, just consider this very interesting point: *the reason you feel the way you do is because you care, otherwise you wouldn't feel like it. This makes you a 'decent' human being. When you look at it like that, it's easy to see that the only individuals who **should** feel guilt (or shame or embarrassment) are those who never do. They **don't** care.*

You might have carried out some deliberate act that you now regret; you might have accidentally caused somebody a serious problem; you might have been accidentally involved with something that you now believe you should have been aware of earlier... But whatever it was, beating yourself up about it won't change it. When something has happened, it can never be *un*happened, no matter how much you want it to be. So you have only a few options – and do be sure to choose one of them, or something else if you can find one that works better for you:

1. Find a way of making amends if possible.
2. Giving money or time to a charity as penance.
3. Accept that a mistake is a mistake, not a crime.
4. Accept that the secret is yours forever.
5. Beat yourself up for the rest of your life.

Now, if you've chosen number 5, Congratulations! You've completed one of the most difficult of tasks – you've established why you're depressed and also that you have no intention of making any changes! So you can now put this book away or perhaps give it to somebody else and get on with living your life the way you have chosen.

That might sound sarcastic or harsh, but in fact, it's the complete truth. You *cannot* hold two opposing ideas in your mind at once and you have chosen the one associated with misery. It might not be the total cause of the depression, but it will definitely maintain it. When you think about it, if you're going to beat yourself up forever you cannot ever *like* yourself (always difficult for the one who suffers depression anyway) and if you don't like yourself, you will believe nobody else likes you and you will become... depressed. That all sounds a little bit like catastrophisation but in this case, it's not. In this case, it's a statement of a psychological fact: you must like yourself before you can accept that anybody else does.

But you probably didn't choose number 5. You probably chose one of the others and whichever one it was, you now have a plan. You might not find it easy to implement yet, but having a plan is a great salve for that subconscious of yours, which cannot *abide* lack of action. You have taken another tiny little step forward to freedom. As a matter of interest, most people would choose either number 3 or 4 – and they work well, because in each case, you are taking full responsibility for your actions and carrying the cost. Now it's no longer part of your catastrophi- sation and you can just let it go.

What's not

The final part of this chapter is a look at an invisible habit which won't, on its own, cause depression but it can certainly add to it. The habit is always looking for what is not, rather than what *is*. And, of course, you always find what you're looking for, so that subconscious of yours will conclude that the world is a rather empty sort of place, devoid of the things that might give you a bit of a lift. We've actually touched upon this before, in Chapter Three. It was where you were asked if you would look to see if you felt better after somebody gave you a self-help idea, or if you would check to see if you were still depressed. In other words looking for it not to have worked.

You might possibly still be doing that, as a matter of fact. If so, instead of looking to see if what you have read so far has helped you, you've been checking to see if you were still as depressed. If not, that's a good thing indeed, so top marks and you can now skip to the end of the chapter, to the 'Personality' heading. On the other hand, if you've just discovered that you're still doing the same thing, don't despair – you just needed a bit of reminding and that's not at all an uncommon circumstance where depression is concerned. And now you're alerted to it, you can begin to **consciously** change the habit and start instead to look for what is. In fact, you can start that right at this very moment by looking to see if you've managed to learn the 'breathing thing' well enough to do it without looking it up.

- If you have – good. That's something you didn't know at the beginning of this book so it's evidence of improvement.
- If you haven't – good. You've just looked to see if something **is**, rather than **is not.** The fact that you discovered it was not is unimportant. It's the fact that you searched for a *positive* that matters.

Easy, wasn't it?

Personality

The way your personality works comes strongly into play where depression is concerned, not just in the way it might contribute to the problem but also how it shows you the best way out of it. It also reveals whether you are more prone to pessimism or optimism, to reactive or active responses, and a whole lot more besides. It will alert you to your natural resources that you can use instinctively and to those that need just a little more effort to use effectively – and even show you how to do just that.

It's one of the most exciting parts of the book!

Chapter Six

It's not what you think (but the way that you think it)

Before continuing with this chapter it's important to complete the questionnaires in Chapter Three, if you've not already done so. Check your answers again, too, to make sure they are as honest as possible, and don't give a thought to what others would say if they knew how you were answering. As has been mentioned before, it's not their life you are seeking to change but yours, and you'll make a better job of that if you don't have any interference – even virtual interference – from others.

It is a fact that the vast majority of people don't really know who they truly are and those who do are usually wrong! This sounds to be a ridiculous statement of course but the fact is that most of us spend a huge amount of time trying to be the way we believe we *should* be, which is often the way we've been taught was 'right', usually during childhood.

But there's a problem here. We're taught that way of being by people who want us to behave in a certain manner for their own ends. There's nothing unfair or nasty about this – in fact it's astonishingly normal. Our teachers (which include our parents) make the mistake of assuming that we are blank slate onto which they can imprint a programme for life... yet nothing could be further from the truth. Everybody, when they're born, is a totally unique human being with totally unique DNA, which governs not just their physical characteristics but their psychology as well. And whatever 'training' we are given by our elders is interpreted according to our understanding of it – which is governed by our basic psychological make-up. This is why siblings brought up in the same way by the same parents in the same circumstances will usually end up being quite different people from each other, with different attitudes, likes and dislikes, moods and manners. It's even possible that one will have a totally different moral code to the other(s) and this can be a constant source of puzzlement to parents, though it never seems to surprise them that their children look physically different from each other.

All this is because of the odd situation that genetic inheritance is random – it skips generations and it might even be the case that you have active genes which are completely dormant in other members of your family. Maybe one person and only one person in your family has curly hair, or a craggy chin; perhaps some are athletic and others are determined couch potatoes; or some might excel at scientific pursuits where others are more into art.

When you're a child you know nothing of all this of course. All you know is what your teachers seem to expect of you. Or, more precisely, you know that they seem to expect *something* of you, and then you get these lessons:

1. When you do what they want you to do, it meets with approval, so you learn the need to do what others want even if you don't know why.
2. If there's some sort of punishment involved when you don't get it right, you learn that it's a *bad thing* not to do what others want.
3. If punishment is meted out when you do something they didn't want you to do, even if you didn't know that, you learn that you're 'not allowed' to have or do what you want.

You might have already worked out that it's impossible to say what effect any of those three circumstances would have on any one individual because it would depend entirely on their particular psychology! Some might remain what we laughingly call 'normal', others might be rebellious, excessively compliant, angry, keen to exert discipline, automatically nurturing... or depressed. And the more specific the 'thing' that was wanted or not wanted, the stronger the response we encounter and the more profound the effect it has upon us. Take sex, for example. Now *there's* a thorny area which almost everybody falls foul of in some way or another. Especially males... But that's another story!

You're probably getting the idea now that the way in which life has overlaid its various influences on top of the unique person you were when you were born has a lot to answer for. And you're right. It would still hold true even if you had a genetic disposition towards depression (which is actually quite rare and usually results in an unchanging low mood which used to have the wonderfully archaic title of 'Melancholia'.) At the root of it all is the age-old battle between nature and nurture and we'll be having a good look at that later on, as well as at how you can reset a large part of your original 'basic blueprint'. First, though, it's important to discover the conflicts that exist in your psyche (that's a posh way of saying your 'mind and personality', remember) as a result of all the lessons that have been handed out in your direction so far.

Personal style

You can think of personality as the way you interact with the world and it is not so much the real self, but the self that has been created by the process of living. We're going to have a look at the three major types – actually there are far more, but these three cover every possible style of human behaviour. It's important to recognise that:

- You've already revealed your underlying personality.
- Very few people are a 'pure' type but will be a combination of all three.
- It's likely that one of the three 'parts' has been suppressed in your case.

You're soon to discover what the questions you've already answered have revealed about you but first, here's a basic description of each type, each 'part' of your psychological make-up. They're the result of the research carried out in the mid 1990s by the author of this programme and the understanding of which has helped so many people all over the world. They are:

- **The Warrior.** The Warrior personality has probably descended from the ancient warrior tribes and has inherited a deep need to be in control of their life. Practical and down to earth, they don't like 'airy-fairy' nonsense and they don't suffer fools gladly, if at all. They can be charming when it suits them as long as there's a good reason to be so – the Warrior seldom does anything for no purpose. In negative mode, they might be extremely loud in an argument and quite critical, and they almost *never* forget a slight, bearing a grudge for years. They are excellent leaders and planners, paying meticulous attention to detail and are quick to spot the flaws in any plan. They are not a 'charisma orientated' person and aren't too concerned about the opinions of others.

- **The Nomad.** Descended directly from the original hunter-gatherer tribes, the modern Nomad must always have something 'going on' – it doesn't matter much whether it's something good or something 'bad'. In fact, this personality will often enjoy the drama of a disaster. They will constantly seek to be the centre of attention or conversation, although they might have no conscious knowledge of this. They won't necessarily travel the land like their ancestors, instead having a tendency to change houses, jobs, partners, cars and almost anything else. Negatively, they can be shallow and somewhat irresponsible; against that, they can lift the spirits of others with boundless enthusiasm, optimism and energy. They make amazing friends and lovers as long as not too much is expected of them.

- **The Settler.** The Settler has inherited the need to be loved and looked after. They like togetherness and sharing and they take their name from the individuals who formed the first settlements, some 10,000 years or so ago, when they ceased to wander the land as hunter-gatherers. They are the world's 'people people' always seeking, and usually finding, the best in others. They can be over-trusting but also forgiving. Negatively, they can be easily upset and might drop into a silent mood which they will refuse to explain, insisting that everything is 'fine' even when it's abundantly clear that it isn't. They are wonderful homemakers, nurturers, carers and listeners, with an intuitive under-standing of the needs of others. One of their biggest diffi-culties is concern over what others think of them, which can cause them a sleepless night now and again.

Who are you?

There's no 'best' one of three types. Each one has their own strengths and weaknesses and the ideal situation is to be able to live your life in the style that suits you best. It's likely, of course, that you've attempted to work out who you are from those descriptions, above. It's even possible that you've decided that one of them is 'you'. But that could be based on what you want others to think about you, not on what you actually are, and if you tried to adopt that mode it's unlikely that you could sustain it for very long.

It's an interesting fact that the Nomad will often claim to be a Warrior, the Settler is usually frightened of the Warrior and the Warrior doesn't really think much at all about the other two!

But no matter what you're thinking right now, you're about to discover what the answers you gave in Chapter Three say about you. We've used the way you respond to the world to assess your *most likely* personality type and the answers you gave will also help you to discover the amount of influence from the other two types. That's actually quite important because it will indicate what you are able to do and how much effort you would have to put in to do it, which will help you greatly in some of the later exercises in the programme. To double check, there's a brief personality test later which will help to confirm your type. Before that, though, let's look at what your previous answers say.

- **Q2/1, W1, B1** = Warrior
- **Q2/2, W2, B2** = Nomad
- **Q2/3, W3, B3** = Settler

Now, of course you might not be so consistent that you have answers like that – most people aren't and it's the numbers rather than the letters that tell you most. Every '1' shows Warrior, '2' shows Nomad and '3' shows Settler. It doesn't matter which order they're in, only how many there are, so if you have two '1' counts you are mostly Warrior and the third number will show you the secondary part of your personality. So, for instance, **Q2/1, W1, B3** would show that you are a Warrior with underlying Settler, while **Q2/2, W2, B1** indicates Nomad with underlying Warrior. Just in case you're still not sure, there's a table at the end of this chapter where you can just look up who you are according to your 'formula'.

You might have discovered that you seem to be a combination personality and this could well be the case. It means that you can use the resources of each type but might not be able to *fully* harness the strength of any one of them, in which case, a 'decider question' is needed to get you focussed onto the main energies available to you, because even in a true combination personality, there is always a slight dominance to one of the three. First, think about the part of you that you call 'I' or 'Me' – you might remember reading about that in Chapter One. Now here's the decider question; what it indicates is shown on the last page of this chapter but do answer the question first, to avoid accidental bias, choosing which answer *feels best*.

Where does that part of you 'live' in your body?:

(a) **Your head**
(b) **You don't really know, OR maybe in an aura around you somehow**
(c) **Your heart or torso**

When you've decided, look it up to see what it says about you...

Strengths and weaknesses

So now you've probably discovered who you were designed to be, even if it somehow doesn't seem to 'fit' at this stage. If that's the case, don't worry about it or worse, decide to change some of your answers (unless you didn't answer them honestly in the first place!) All it means is that you've been trying to be somebody else, and that might even be part of the reason for the depression. Possibly even the main reason. Not a problem if so, because you will soon be able to start sorting *that* out.

First, though, we'll have a look at the main strengths and weaknesses of each personality type:

- **Warrior** (positive): Observant, determined, tenacious, good planner, quick to spot errors, sensible, assertive, practical, security-minded.
- **Warrior** (negative): Controlling, manipulative, aggressive, critical, blunt.
- **Nomad** (positive): Lively, enthusiastic, optimistic, energetic, inventive, individualistic, up-beat, entertaining, tireless.
- **Nomad** (negative): Irresponsible, dramatic, unreliable, shallow, show-off.
- **Settler** (positive): Kind, caring, intuitive, reliable,

thoughtful, cheerful, communicative, good listener, 'people person'.

- **Settler** (negative): Moody, doormat, martyr, drab, weak.

Very few people will exhibit every aspect of behaviour listed there, and very few people will show only positive traits. At the moment, in fact, it's likely that you don't really show any of them very clearly if at all... depression's like that, stopping so much of personality from exhibiting itself. But where you recognise that you have a tendency towards a particular negative 'way of being', you can now begin to accept that there's nothing nasty about it – it's a totally natural aspect of the way you are 'designed'. This does *not* mean, however, that it's perfectly all right to indulge it (unless you don't care about upsetting others); it's more the case that you need to rein it in most of the time. We all have to control *some* of our urges, if we want to get on with others in the best way possible.

Now, it might seem to you as if you're being asked to control some part of your personality immediately after being told that you need to be yourself! To an extent, that's true... but it's only those *negative* aspects that you need to get a grip of, since doing that allows you the best chance of being likeable to others. If you want to be, of course.

It's worth knowing that it's when you're under pressure of any sort that you will be most likely to exhibit the major part of your personality type, the bit before the forward slash mark in the table – *Warrior*, for instance, if you're 'Warrior/Nomad' or 'Warrior/Settler'. The rest of the time, you will probably just 'go with the flow', sometimes showing your major type, sometimes the secondary, as the situation encourages. In either case you can create a more positive personal approach to life that will help to keep you more focussed and *alive*. It's an easy task to perform, though just like the 'but reversal' exercise in Chapter Four, it needs practice in order to overcome force of habit. In this instance, the habit is of showing depression instead of your personality, so change is due! To start with, look at the positive attributes listed as being part of your primary personality type. Choose the one you like best, and even if you've never considered before that it was anything to do with you, adopt it as being a major part of your personal style (if you like it, it will definitely be right for you.) Having chosen, think of an event that happened recently – it doesn't matter what – and the way you reacted with it. Now go through it in your mind again but this time bringing that attribute to bear and imagining how you might have behaved differently.

Perhaps you were tenacious or observant; optimistic and energetic maybe; or thoughtful and communicative. Whatever you were in your mind, if you did the exercise correctly, you were **participating.** *Yes, it was 'only' in your thoughts but when did you last do anything like it, even just in your thoughts? It's an improvement!*

Remember, it's only an exercise. You don't have to go out and actually do it, so it's safe to imagine it as vividly as you possibly can. And if you want to do the 'deluxe' version of the exercise, repeat it several times, imagining yourself behaving and inter-acting each time in a different style, including the negatives. If you're a Nomad, for instance, you can imagine being: *lively, enthusiastic, optimistic, energetic, inventive, individualistic, up-beat, entertaining, tireless,* as well as: *irresponsible, dramatic, unreliable, shallow, a show-off.* This is a work out for the personality and will do you no end of good!

Before we move on to another 'thought experiment' there's one more task to perform but it only applies if you have identified yourself as a 'whole' Warrior, Settler or Nomad. It's desirable to have an 'offset' from that totality, so choose a positive attribute that strongly appeals to you from one of the other two groups and 'adopt' it as your own. It's likely, since you find it appealing, that it actually is a part of the way you're made anyway – it just didn't appear as a result of the questions you've answered. Recognise and accept that the group it come from is your secondary personality so you can place it after the forward slash mark – and let yourself accept that this is your real personality, be it Warrior/Settler, Nomad/Warrior, Settler/Nomad or any other combination. Now you're ready to move on to a powerful personal development process that has helped many thousands of people all over the world.

The VMI

'VMI' stands for 'Vivid Mental Image' and it's what you're going to create to help you strengthen the new identity that you have started creating for yourself. This is a technique that is frequently used by therapists to help create positive change in the mind. It can work extraordinarily well because the physical brain will accept imagination as a form of reality as long as what is being imagined doesn't conflict with other ideas that are already held in the mind. As a matter of interest, this is why 'giving yourself a good talking to' usually makes no lasting change, if any at all... the subconscious already has the idea that whatever you're talking about is difficult and should not be avoided if possible.

So we have to be a little more subtle. We have to create the idea of what's needed without going head on at it, and the VMI is an ideal method. This exercise is in three sections of two parts each, and in each section you do the first part with your eyes open, the second part with eyes closed. So let's get to work straight away!

Warrior Part 1

For the first part of the first section, you're going to imagine what an ancient Warrior might be like, even if 'Warrior' isn't an obvious part of your profile – the personality tests have shown the *most active* parts of your personality, not the *only* parts! Everybody has something of all three types. It's best to do these exercises on your own, by the way, so you can keep determinedly to what *you* think, and can't be persuaded by somebody else that you're getting it wrong. The only way you could get it wrong, in fact, would be by listening to somebody else telling you what you should be thinking...

So, your Warrior can be somebody from thousands of years ago or only a couple of centuries back. It might be an individual from a foreign land or from your own country. The important thing is that it must be a creation of your own imagination, not somebody you know or a character from a film – if you were to choose something like that you would be 'role modelling' and while that has it's place, it's nowhere near as powerful as what we're doing here.

As for what sort of Warrior, you might choose to imagine an ancient oriental like a Han Archer or a Samurai. You could find yourself thinking of a Native American, or a prehistoric tribal chief. Roman Centurions, Norsemen, Vikings, Celtic Chieftains, Zulus, Egyptian Pharaohs, Navy Captains or Army leaders, infantry, cavalry or foot soldiers are all acceptable. The great-great Grandfather of whom you've seen a photograph in his army uniform isn't. Nor is anybody else that you've seen in a photograph, come to that. Characters in films are out, too, even if they're depicting something from hundreds of years ago. This needs to be an image you've conjured up from the depths of your imagination and it doesn't matter if it takes a while. The depression will wait and might even begin to weaken its grip a little while you're thinking. You might find yourself at this moment doing an 'Arbut': *"Ah but I can't visualise, you see, so I just can't see things in my mind's eye."*

Not exactly true...

If it were, you wouldn't have the vaguest idea what a Warrior even *was*. But you've read this far so you must have some idea, and however those ideas appear in your mind is what visualisation is *to you*. If it feels like you're just *thinking* of a Warrior in some way, that's all you need to do. So when you're asked to imagine something, just think of it. It will work every bit as well as if you were the most powerful visualiser on the planet. So now think of 'your' Warrior. See/sense/think/feel:

- What sort of Warrior
- Male or female
- How old
- What they are wearing
- Colour of their skin
- Colour of their hair
- How they sound
- How they smell
- How they feel to the touch
- How they move
- What it is that shows they are a Warrior – a weapon, facial expression, clothing, or anything else that clearly states 'I am a Warrior'
- If they have a name (can be just 'Warrior')

Write those things down and you're nearly done for this first part. A good description might be something like: *Ancient Greek (like a God), male, thirties, white tunic with a broad gold belt, tanned, blonde, determined, smells like herbs, firm-bodied, moves like an athlete, Warrior.* That description makes the character just about as real as it can get – and if you want to, you can add anything else to the description... but don't leave anything out. If you find it difficult at first, practising describing somebody you know (from memory) will help – and do be sure that you create a *positive* Warrior, not a tyrant or a despot!

Warrior, Part 2

Now for the second part, the true VMI work... First, do the 'breathing thing' with your eyes closed until you find that quiet 'moment of now' you discovered in Chapter Four. When you have it, see/sense/think or feel the individual you have created in your mind like a real person or perhaps a video. If it begins to change in some way from what you've written down, just go along with that, updating your written description later, because it means your subconscious is seeking to create a more suitable 'you' Warrior. Make it as vivid as you can, and if you are able to use your mind well enough, it might even begin to feel as if you know this person from somewhere. Keep the image or thought in your mind for as long as you can, and when it fades (which it will), allow your eyes to open. You don't need to do anything else at this stage.

Now, if you feel you just weren't very good at all that, which is quite usual if you suffer depression, don't worry! Give yourself a bit of praise for even having attempted it in the first place, then be content in the knowledge that it's not how well you did the exercise that is so important but that you actually did it. You made your brain and mind work differently from the way they usually do. You've created positive change, even if you can't feel much of it at the moment.

Nomad, Part 1

Before you move on to this exercise, give yourself a few minutes' break, so that you can give each exercise the concentration it deserves. If you found the first one difficult or tiring, then put the book down for a little while, even a day or so, and come back to it when you're ready.

The exercise for the Nomad is the same as for Warrior except, of course, that you're going to choose a different image. The same rules apply though, in that it must be an image of somebody from at least a couple of hundred years ago, though might be a lot further back than that. Suitable Nomad images are: Actors, orators, illusionists, salesmen, entertainers, sailors, Bedouin, minstrels, wizards, gypsy, juggler. Anybody who seeks to be 'different from the crowd' in a positive manner or anybody who is inspirational is a good Nomad character. As before, you need to create a description that brings this part of your personality to life, using the same list as for the Warrior. To save you looking back, here's the list again:

- What sort of Nomad
- Male or female
- How old
- What they are wearing
- Colour of their skin
- Colour of their hair
- How they sound
- How they smell
- How they feel to the touch
- How they move
- What it is that shows their Nomad status – as with the Warrior, this can be anything at all that makes the 'this is who I am' statement
- If they have a name (can be just 'Nomad')

Create a detailed description and write it down, just as you did before, and ensuring a positively-orientated individual, somebody personable, energetic and lively, not irresponsible and unreliable!

Nomad, Part 2

This is exactly the same exercise as for the Warrior, using the 'breathing thing' first to find that quiet 'moment of now', then creating a dynamically active image, somebody you can almost sense as a real person. Make it vivid, holding it in your mind until it fades, as before. Again, there's no need to do anything else at this stage, and you shouldn't worry if it just doesn't seem to come as easily as you might have thought. Just the attempt at the exercise is enough for your needs here.

Settler, Part 1

As before, you should allow yourself a short break before continuing, or even leave the next exercise until the next day if you've tired yourself.

All the same rules as for the Warrior and Nomad apply here, which you are probably anticipating. The Settler needs to be a community minded individual, somebody who is happy being part of a team without the need to seek to be the centre of attention. Examples of suitable Settlers are: Farmers, teachers, Pilgrim Fathers, seamstresses, nurses, angels, veterinarians, caregivers, hand maidens, builders, land workers. Anybody who is in some way supportive of others or provides a service to their community or tribe is a good model here.

As before, write down your description, being as detailed as you can, and do make sure that this is a character who is *slightly* 'larger than life', even if that feels distinctly out of character for you, which it might.

Settler, Part 2

Conduct exactly the same exercise as for the Warrior and Nomad. Now you have just one more task before your VMI work is complete...

Energising

The final part of the VMI work is what will help you to make a steady but continuous change in the way you are and the way you feel, almost without having to do anything. You've already done some of the work, selecting the attributes that appeal to you from the lists; to make certain you are ready to commence this final stage, choose the attributes you like best from the positive ones of each type. For instance, you might end up with *Determined, Optimistic, Intuitive* or maybe: *Observant, Inventive, Thoughtful*. Remember to choose the attributes you like best, not simply the ones that you think are easier to put into practice, or those that you think won't draw negative comment from others.

If we are to get you feeling good about yourself and good about life, it's important that you start to claim the personal self you truly are.

You will probably find it easier to select the attribute associated with your primary personality than with the other two, which is completely normal – but still make sure that it's what you like best about that type. For instance, you might like 'assertive' from the Warrior attributes but wonder about choosing it because you've never been able to be assertive... but if you like it, choose it! The fact that you like it indicates that you can be it; if that were not the case, it would not concern you at all that you were not very assertive – you probably wouldn't like assertiveness at all – and it would be one of the other attributes that grabbed your attention.

So, now you have your three-word description of the basic 'you' (because that's what it is) and the next task is to prepare your mind and brain to be able to live it! You've already done all the hard work and this part is really just the 'icing on the cake', working in the same manner as you did in the second part of each VMI creation, with one small difference...

Read the process through a couple of times first, because you will be doing this with your eyes closed, so you'll need to remember it. Once you've used the 'breathing thing' to find the quiet moment of now, first of all find a memory of an event of some sort that left you feeling uncomfortable. It doesn't matter what sort of uncomfortable, as long as it has a definite feeling about it, so you can use the same one you chose earlier if you wish. Now conjure up the image of your primary personality type (just for clarification, that's the part before the forward slash mark in 'Warrior/Nomad', for example), followed by the other two in any order. See them standing behind the main 'part' and know in your mind that they're there to provide support. When you're ready, play through the uncomfortable event as a bystander observing how the team of three handle the situation, the leader receiving support and back up as necessary via the resources of the other two. They might provide ideas, suggest a change of approach, confirm a course of action or anything else that's needed.

When you've played it through enough to be familiar with it, let one of the other two take the lead and see how that feels as you observe the same event, then finally have the third one taking charge. Remember, this is only a thought exercise so you can be as inventive as you like, because there's no chance of any awkwardness occurring! Finally, run through everything again but this time playing it as yourself with those three resources comfortably active. The secret with this exercise is to work at it until it's completely comfortable and begins to feel as if it's something that somehow 'belongs' to you – because it does.

Have you got all that? Good – *do it now!*

Over the next few days and weeks, you can repeat this exercise with any event you like, whether it's recent or from the distant past. If it happened only yesterday, that's fine; if it happened twenty years ago and you've only just remembered it, that's fine too. And it's still fine if it's something you've known about all along but have never really managed to face before. The more events you review like that, the stronger the change to the way you see yourself will become – but it does need to be worked at, just like anything else we want to achieve!

In the next chapter, we're going to be investigating some other invisible thought processes, and when we shine some light on them you'll be surprised at what you find there...

Table of Personality Types

Q2/1, W1 with: **B1** = Warrior; **B2** = Warrior/Nomad, **B3** = Warrior/Settler

Q2/1, W2 with: **B1** = Warrior/Nomad; **B2** = Nomad/Warrior; **B3** = Combination

Q2/1, W3 with: **B1** = Warrior/Settler; **B2** = Combination; **B3** = Settler/Warrior

Q2/2, W1 with: **B1** = Warrior/Nomad; **B2** = Nomad/Warrior; **B3** = Combination

Q2/2, W2 with: **B1** = Nomad/Warrior; **B2** = Nomad; **B3** = Nomad/Settler

Q2/2, W3 with: **B1** = Combination; **B2** = Nomad/Settler; **B3** = Settler/Nomad

Q3/W1 with: **B1** = Warrior/Settler; **B2** = Combination; **B3** = Settler/Warrior

Q3/W2 with: **B1** = Combination; **B2** = Nomad/Settler; **B3** = Settler/Nomad

Q3/W3 with: **B1** = Settler/Warrior; **B2** = Settler/Nomad; **B3** = Settler

'Decider' question if needed: (a) = **Warrior; (b)** = **Nomad; (c)** = **Settler**

If you are any of the Combination classifications, then your personality type will be one of the following:

Warrior/Combination, Nomad/Combination, Settler/Combination

*NB: This personality test was designed especially for those people who suffer from depression and want to get better. The results might not be accurate for individuals who do **not** suffer from depression or do not want to get better.*

Looking Back

Discovering hidden truths

One of the most difficult things for the depressed person to take on board is that they don't know the truth about themselves or their life. It can so easily look as if almost everybody else is comfortable with their life and that they don't have any problems. That, though, is an illusion. It certainly seems realistic but it's an illusion nonetheless. How you feel and how others seem are completely different concepts – when you try to compare them, you are really looking at yourself twice. Once as **you** currently are, the second time as how *you believe* they are… or maybe how you believe you would be if you had their life.

Interestingly, it's highly likely that if you knew beyond doubt that nobody felt better than you or had a better life than you, you would immediately start to feel better. In the Second World War, doctors discovered that cases of depression dropped by 90%, even though there was a war raging and people were being killed. But of course, everybody was in the same boat.

So let's start to find the hidden truths that are vital to get you on course for a better life in the future!

Chapter Seven

Getting the best out of looking back

Before you begin reading this chapter, grab yourself a pen and paper because you need to write down your answers to some questions later. There are only a few but if you simply try to remember all your responses, you'll soon become thoroughly confused! Not only that, you'll probably hinder your chances of getting the result you want from this book, as you'll soon see.

Before we get to that part, though, it's worth considering something that we've already had a little look at, though this phrase sums it up nicely:

"Whether you think you can or think you can't, you're probably right."
Henry Ford

What Mr Ford was saying in an extremely succinct way was that what you think governs what you get. The reason for this is that the subconscious mind is at the same time powerful, very complex and ridiculously simple. Complex and powerful in that it works far faster than your conscious thinking processes and just won't be interfered with, yet simple in that it blindly follows a task without any consideration as to whether it's what you consciously want or not.

Here's an example of the way it works: *you **consciously** want to have a good time on a holiday but fear that depression will get in the way and spoil it for everyone else. The fear creates a stronger imagined outcome than the wish, and because it's stronger the subconscious views it as the most important task and so responds to it. It's the way we're designed...*

It's all down to those ancestors of ours again. Although

survival was more precarious for them than it is for us, their life was far simpler overall. Each individual had a task to perform and life was pretty much the same for all of them, the main aspiration being to survive. If they managed that they were doing fine, if not... well, they were hardly in a position to get upset about it. And so it was, that evolution favoured those with the fastest and most vivid instincts embedded into their subconscious processes. And everything was just as it should be, then. They thought about what they *wanted* to happen (and probably drew pictures on cave walls about it as well) and because the alternative could possibly be death, they thought strongly about avoiding that outcome in any way they could. If life went as planned, everything was good. If not, there wasn't any life to think about

Now fast-forward a couple of hundred thousand years or so... There's suddenly a great deal more to think about than survival, in particular the idea we've been given of how life *should* be. Our ancestors were taught nothing of the sort. Their lessons came from the elders of the tribe and we're going to look at what was likely to be the five most important things they had to learn:

1. If somebody or something is a threat, try to kill it before it kills you
2. Do what the elders do because they've survived so they know best
3. You're not special unless you *do something* special
4. Anybody of the preferred gender is a potential mate
5. How you look is not important. What you do *is*

Of course, there would have been a few more rules than that, though likely to have been just as 'black and white'. If we look at a similar set of rules today though, things are vastly different, and not only that, they're not all experience-based from the elders. Some of them come from your peers, with no more experience of living than you have, and what they try to 'teach' is likely to be biased in their personal favour, rather than being for the good of the tribe. So while you are becoming an adult, you are taught things like:

1. If something or somebody is a threat, be careful how you deal with it or you'll probably be the one getting punished. On the other hand, any form of restriction is unfair and you should be able to do exactly as you like
2. The older generation don't know what they're doing, so they have to be challenged and maybe sneered at
3. If you're not automatically amazing, you're a failure
4. Anybody of the preferred gender has to be of suitable social class, within the right age-group, and must be accepted by your friends and family
5. How you look governs how well you get on. You have to look amazing

The modern rules are a lot more complicated than those our ancestors had to abide by... but your subconscious doesn't take any account of that. Evolution moves very slowly indeed and the subconscious still views failure as a threat to survival, so it will attempt to complete whatever is the strongest task in your mind. There was really only one negative thought our ancestors had and that was that they might die if they got their plans wrong. That's a great incentive to keep focussed totally on what you want to happen. Most of the time now, though, the negative thought does *not* involve dying so the subconscious can just go with whatever gives it the most vivid message. It simply doesn't know or care if what it gets is a good thing or a bad thing.

You're probably way ahead of the book now!

It's interesting that the majority of people who comply with as many of the rules as possible without questioning them will get what they think they will get. If they don't, most of them manage to have another go, or accept that 'the time wasn't right' or some other mitigating circumstance designed to offset their disappointment. Somehow, they get through life reasonably unscathed and manage to be at ease, or almost at ease, with their lot. But not everybody. Some just find it tougher than others and begin to suffer all sorts of problems... including depression. As to the question of why this difference exists, well, there's no easy answer. It might be to do with upbringing – and there's more about that in the next chapter – or maybe personality, or some other reason. Fortunately, we don't need to find out why; we have just one task to perform and that is to get you thinking about, and vividly imagining, exactly what you want instead of what you fear.

Regrets

Regret is an insidious and self-sustaining concept. It's easy to regret all sorts of things; not making more effort, the failed relationships and missed opportunities, the lack of support when you needed it, and so on. It can so easily be coupled with the ultimate expression of regret: *"It's too late for me now..."* when it then starts to act as a self-fulfilling prophecy. Remember, your subconscious will seek to achieve that which you appear to want and the 'too late' statement is an instruction to accept that there is never going to be any beneficial change. In fact, there's only one useful thing you can do with regret.

Stop it!

It locks you into the past and even brings the past forward with you. It colours what you believe you can and cannot do and so will lead to more of itself at every opportunity. The unsullied future, which is yours to do with as you wish, hurtles past you almost unnoticed while you're busy regretting the unchangeable events of the past and believing that all you will find is more of the same. It achieves nothing useful, so let's set about dropping the whole notion, allowing you to recognise the future for what it is – a totally clean slate without any preconceived plan or idea about how you should or should not be, what you can or cannot do. We'll get on to the 'meat' of the work shortly but there's some preparation to do first...

The preparation is in the form of a neat little trick that on its own can create amazing change to the way you automatically think. To start, answer this simple question:

What direction do you instinctively feel your 'line of life' flows in?
(a) From one side of you to the other (either right to left or left to right)
(b) From back to front (from behind you to in front of you)

If you answer is (b) then you don't need to do anything more and you can skip to the next section **'Looking back'**. Since you're still reading, though, you have a task to perform – don't worry, because it's easy and will almost certainly make a drastic improvement in the way you view not just your life but all of life generally. **Read through what you're going to do first**, then do the 'breathing thing' before you actually do it with your eyes closed. Currently, your life is running from one side of you to the other – it doesn't really matter which way, because it still means that your past and all the uncomfortable stuff that has been part of it is coming along with you, next to you. It means you could almost see it out of the corner of your eye. Not only that, but your future is on the other side of you, level with you but still not clearly visible – so you can't see clearly where you're going!

It's all very unhelpful, so let's do something about it straight away. First, decide what colour your lifeline is; it can be any colour that just feels right to you and ideally it will have an energy of some sort. It doesn't have to be like a wide path because it's only a guide to the direction of life. For instance, if you thought of an electric blue, thin wire, that was somehow alive and vibrating, that would do just fine. A dull-looking path or walkway wouldn't be so good. A vivid orange or red thread would be good but a knotted rope would not work very well at all. Let your imagination be as wild as you like and make your 'lifeline' as vivid as you possibly can – the more energetic and lively you can make it (even if you are usually not!) the better it will work.

When you've done the 'breathing thing' and found the 'now moment', see in your mind's eye, (or just think of) that lifeline running in its usual direction. Then do whatever it takes to get it to run from back to front. You might be able to just think it there; you might need to imagine one of your VMI figures (probably the Warrior) helping you, or even *all* of your VMI figures assisting; you might even find that you can keep the lifeline running in the same direction that it currently is but turn your body to face along it instead of across it. Whatever it takes... It doesn't matter if it seems that it won't stay there as long as you can get it there in the first place. When you've managed to get it flowing from back to front even only for the shortest time, that's when to open your eyes.

Do it now!

Good. Now the next part of this exercise is to learn to switch that lifeline whenever you decide to, rather than have to go through the whole of the above routine – and all you have to do is practise it a few times. It's unlikely, though not impossible, that you will be able to keep it running from back to front, much more likely that you'll begin to recognise the times when it's useful to make it switch. One such time, of course, is if you catch yourself out dwelling on some past regret or other. Another is when you just don't seem to be able to think about the future without some apprehension. The last two parts of the exercise covers both those situations.

Looking backwards

With your lifeline aligned from back to front, you now have to *choose* to look at the past... And with every second of every day, it's receding further and further behind you and becoming less and less important. But not everything is rubbish and your mind already knows that, which is why it might not have been easy to let go of what has gone and cannot be changed. So you're soon going to discover how to hang on to that which is good and let go of that which is not. As you look back, you might perceive that the line of your life is full of lumps and bumps, cloudy bits, dull bits, and some downright horrendous bits... it's not a pretty sight overall.

Looking forward

But if you now turn and look along the line to your future, it has none of that. It's pristine, unsullied and just waiting for you to make the best of it. It's probably empty at the moment, so let's put something there to improve matters even further. Some way along the line, as far away as you want it to be, place a symbol that represents a time when you know you're getting better. It can be a golden arch, a silver cup, a huge gift-wrapped box... absolutely anything that represents what you truly want to find as a result of the work you're doing with this book. It doesn't have to be an object – it can be a shaft of bright light or a crowd of people all smiling and cheering you on to the finish line. It matters not one jot that you know it's not real. Just make it as vivid as you can so that your mind and brain can understand without any doubt exactly what it is you want. Now, if you're having trouble with any of this, it suggests one of two situations:

1. You haven't completed some of the exercises you've already read, in which case it'd be a really good idea to go back and do them now.

2. A part of you doesn't really want to get better – and that means we're looking at some of the things we talked about in Chapter Three. If that's the case, the best thing would be to have another look at them and see what you can change.

And when all that's done and sorted out, spend a little while just thinking – realistically – about how you want life to be and how you want life to feel when you get to that point where the symbol is. And keep it light! When that's done, you're ready to move on to the next stage of setting yourself free.

Freedom questions

Have you got your pen and paper handy? You're going to need them if you're serious about getting the best possible result from this book because you'll be making notes about your answers to the questions that follow shortly. As always, answer as you truly feel or believe (even if you normally keep that a closely guarded secret) not as you think you *should* feel or believe – that would negate the whole thing. This questionnaire is quite different from those you have already completed and is likely to be more challenging; also, there are no right or wrong answers and no definitive test results for you to investigate afterwards. It's essentially a self-exploration and reality test exercise and the more honest you are the better will be your exploration. It's important that you decide in advance that nobody else will ever be allowed to see your answers, and also important that you write down your response to each question before moving onto the next one. Scanning everything first will definitely skew the results and might even work against you getting better, so for this reason, a 'white gap' is left after each. You need to complete this in one go, so make sure you won't be disturbed for around thirty minutes or so or maybe even a little longer. You won't want to rush.

Question 1: If you had to blame somebody for the depression you experience, who would it be? *(You're not allowed to blame yourself here)*. Think about it for as long as you need to but do write the answer down before continuing. You must name somebody, even if you're not sure why you chose them, even if it seems to be totally unfair for some reason.

Question 2: Does it seem to you that they are *totally* responsible for the feeling of depression or only part of it? Write your answer down.

Question 3: If your answer to Question 2 was 'totally', move on to Question 4. If you wrote 'Partly' then write down who else is in your mind.

Question 4: Why did you choose the person or people in your answers to Questions 1 & 2? Again, think about it as long as you need to but continue before tackling the next question. It doesn't matter if you think the reasons might be unfair as long as they are what you truly believe; it's your thoughts that count, since the depression is powered by your thoughts. It doesn't matter how 'nice' somebody is or tries to be, or what other people think or feel, it's *your* feelings we're working with here, so be honest.

Question 5: Do you believe the person or people you've written down actually intended to hurt you, or was it just a result of the way they are? Also, is that just with you or are they like it with everybody? *(Here, you might answer something like: "It's just the way they are," or: "No – they're just horrid," or perhaps: "It's just with me." If you really don't know, write "I don't know" instead.)*

Question 6: If they meant to hurt you, write down what you believe that says about them. If they're deliberately like that with everybody write down more of what it seems to you that it says about them. If it was just the way they are, write the names of at least three other people they might also have hurt.

Question 7: Have you written down your answers so far? If not, do it now, and also write: *"I need to do more to help myself and I'm already learning why this is important!"*

Question 8: Write down what you believe to be the level of contentment of those you have written about. Classify it as poor, average, or good.

Question 9: When you look (or think) back along your lifeline, notice what sort of colour it seems to be and how it feels. Now change the colour in your mind to any other colour as long as it's *bright*. Write down both feelings and your reaction to the second one – this can be anything from: *surprised*, through *nice, curious, happy* or *weird*, to *irritated* or *angry*.

Question 10: Write down the symbol you placed on your future lifeline in the 'Looking forward' section above – you can change it if you wish. If you do, make a note that it's changed but there's no need to say anything else.

Question 11: This last one is not so much a question as an exercise but it fits in here very well... Ponder for a few moments on the part of the lifeline that is now behind you (or swing it round if necessary.) Find the things you want to keep and write them down. They can be anything; times you won a prize, had a pet, impressed somebody (even if only for a moment or two), fell in love, discovered somebody loved you, bought something you wanted, received a present you weren't expecting... Anything that felt good. Ignore anything that seemed to spoil it later on – there's nothing to be gained from thinking of that. The 'up moment' still happened and is, and always was, still part of your life and still important. Recognise that they are not just memories, but an actual part of *you*. They contribute to the life you are going to find. Write them down, however long it takes, and revel in the fact that they are and always will be part of your life and cannot ever be taken from you. And if you really can't find anything, which is extraordinarily rare, then instead revel in the fact that in spite of all the rubbish, you've survived and you're still fighting. Because you're here.

Now, before you go any further, if you've not written your answers down, *for whatever reason,* you've now highlighted the foundation of the depression. It's one of those truths that might be uncomfortable or extremely irritating... but it's also a fact. You're trapped in an absolutely awful state of grey and leaden misery but **you're not doing your best to escape the trap.** Whether you just couldn't be bothered, felt uncomfortable, worried that somebody might see what you wrote, decided you could do it all in your mind, decided you would do it later, or any other excuse, you avoided the simple task of writing something down. Yes, it takes effort, but life's like that for everybody at some point. Now here's another question for you: if you knew beyond doubt that going back and completing the questionnaire now would *instantaneously* dispel the depression, would you do it? The answer will tell you much!

If you started writing after Question 7, excellent! That indicates that you can at least be 'fired up' into taking action to help yourself. If you started writing straight away, that's obviously the best response and it shows that you are already on the right track. Even if you struggled with some of the answers, even if you're not sure that what you wrote was the truth, you're still on the right track. And even if you had to go back and do the whole thing, you're making progress now. But if you still haven't done it, there's very little point in reading the rest of this book, unless it's just to understand the nature of depression and how it can be resolved when somebody tries.

You still can do something useful for yourself, even at this last minute: take responsibility for the situation and go back to do the questionnaire... **Do it now!**

Stage two

Time for the second stage of this work now, a look at your answers to the questions. First, **Question 1:** However it seems now, the person you wrote down has *something* to do with the depression you feel, or they would not have come into your mind. This is true even if you just chose somebody at random to get through the exercise. Decide that whatever it was they did belongs way back on that line of the past. Put it there and make sure the line is behind you. Do the same exercise with anybody else that came up in **Question 3.** (There's no need to do anything with your answer to **Question 2**, since that was just to get you ready for the next one.)

Question 4: Think about your answer again and decide that life's too short to allow whoever you've named there to continue to control your life. They have their thoughts, you have yours – it's as simple as that. Recognise that their thoughts are about them, what they think, not you. They're only able to tell you what *they* think. You would probably agree instantly that not everybody thinks like you... So you cannot know what was really in their minds. Whatever they did or said was relevant *to* them and *for* them. That's the way we all are, every one of us. If our ancestors had not been at least a little more interested in themselves than anybody else (with very few exceptions), they would not have survived – so we've all inherited that tendency towards self-interest. Put what they did back where the last thing went – way back on that line of the past.

Questions 5 & 6 are inter-related, of course. If you just wrote something along the lines of: *"They didn't like me,"* go back and write something about what they feel about themselves... Because it's that that makes them seek to wound others. When you think of it, why on earth would anybody want to spent time attacking people 'just because'? It's *always* about self!

Question 7: Hopefully, you had already been writing your answers down at this point but if not, did you write: *"I need to do more to help myself and I'm already learning why this is important!"* as was suggested? If you did, good – now smile at the truth of it. When you write something down like that, it uses a different part of the brain from if you just read it – it uses the *Executive Centres* which is the part of you that controls your choices and your behaviour patterns. If you didn't write it the first time, do it now – and then smile as you recognise the truth of it. The smile, by the way, is almost as important as the writing, since it confirms positive acceptance as far as the subconscious is concerned.

Question 8: Write down now how you came to the conclusion you did and also how you can be certain that you were correct. If having to do that changes your mind, then this part of the exercise has been successful! If it doesn't, then you already have all the skills you need to find contentment – you just haven't employed them properly in the past and the book is going to help you no end. Already is helping you, more than likely.

Question 9: If your reaction was 'good' or similar, there's nothing else you need to do, because you've already learnt that perception can change feelings in a positive way. If it was 'bad', however, then explore in your thoughts why that might have been, since it will be a sign of resistance to positive change... After all, if you were truly seeking to feel better, your subconscious would have had you choosing a colour that lifted you! Keep thinking about that until you 'get it' and then do the exercise again. The colour you choose is unimportant; that it lifts your feelings is an indicator that you can accept positive change.

Question 10: If the symbol you chose was a trophy of any kind or a representation of winning, it's probable that you have enough self-sufficiency to succeed by your own efforts and are already well on the way to getting better; if it was a box, bag, or some other container in which you are unaware of the contents, it suggests that you are not quite sure about your abilities – but don't worry, because you will find them when you get there and your subconscious is aware of that; if it's people encouraging or cheering you or in some other way congratulating you, it suggests that you can't do the job *entirely* on your own (many can't) and so you need to let people know what you're up to and enlist their help. Don't make it the same people you mentioned earlier, though!

Question 11 needs no comment since it was an exercise in itself and has already done its work, no matter what you chose.

And that brings us to the end of this chapter. It's probably been the most difficult one so far and those 'Freedom Questions' you've spent ages answering might well have felt like anything but! And yet, if you ponder over them for a while you'll be able to see that they might have alerted you to some 'stuff' and helped you change one or two notions that you might have held for some time. And change of that sort is always good, since understanding is the gateway to freedom... And you're going to find even more of an understanding about self in the next chapter.

Chapter Eight

Nature and Nurture – the biggest F up!

In this chapter, we're going to have a look at the way upbringing can have a devastating effect upon an individual. It's an interesting fact that parents who are loving and caring can make every bit as much of a mess of it as those who weren't really very interested... but they don't know that.

Before we get to that though, it's worth mentioning that most of the exercises you've done so far were not 'one-offs'. They are intended to be practised as often as you need them... because that way, they will continue to chip away at the edges of depression, loosening its hold until it falls away completely. So here's a list, as a reminder:

- The Double-sided Cheval Mirror (Chapter One)
- The 'Act of Will' (Chapter Two)
- The Smile and the High Five (Chapter Two)
- The Deadly Embrace Test (Chapter Three)
- The 'Breathing Thing' (Chapter Four)
- 'But Reversal' (Chapter Four)
- The Virtual World (Chapter Four)
- The "Wait a Minute!" Solution (Chapter Five)
- The Locked Safe (Chapter Five)
- Exercising the Favourite Aspect of Personality (Chapter Six)
- The VMI Exercise (Chapter Six)
- The Lifeline Exercise (Chapter Seven)

They don't *all* have to be practised every day, of course, but neither should any one of them be totally ignored... unless and until you've become so familiar with them and can do them so easily, they've become boring.

The templates of life

Now we're going to investigate one of the most controversial subjects in the whole world of human behaviour, whether nature or nurture is what makes the man... so we'll start at the beginning. When you were born, you came equipped with a brain template which was essentially a set of hard-wired patterns and responses to cope with the world. The only instinctive responses that would be evident at that time are to do with being startled and falling. But there was a whole lot more there in an embryonic form, including the bit we're most interested in – your basic personality. How you cope with the input from your five senses, along with your responses to perceived stimuli like frustration, waiting, being handled, rejection, movement, manipulation, clothing, restriction, discomfort... and more besides.

That template was, in effect, a plan for the life you were 'designed' to lead. We'll call it the 'Ego Ideal' template – EI from now on – because it's associated with the set of responses that would be perfect for your sense of self. But then life happened and almost immediately a different template had to start forming – a brain pattern associated with experience. We can call that the 'As Is' template – or AI for easiness – and at the beginning it was the same as the EI template. But it wasn't long before you began to discover that although you knew you were the centre of existence, the others around you didn't always seem to share the same opinion. You might demand to be fed but it didn't happen as fast as you wanted it to; or perhaps there was insistence on feeding when you really didn't want that at all. Not at that moment anyway. You might want to sleep or be awake but others had other ideas and gradually you began to discover an uncomfortable truth – you were not in control of your world.

Now, as an aside here, there are many people who would disagree with what you've just been reading. And yet, if you ask any parent with two or more children how quickly they knew that the second was different from the first, they will almost always say 'immediately'. (The only time they won't is on the very rare occasion when there wasn't actually any difference.) Everybody is totally unique, totally unlike any other human that has ever been born – that's to do with the infinite number of different connections of neurons in the brain and too complex to talk about here. The important thing, though, is that while parents might pay lip service to the idea, they do something very odd... They try to make the child become just like them! Some of their teaching is completely necessary of course to allow us to exist in the hugely complex society that is humanity. But whether it's necessary of just one of those 'because I say so' things, the effect is the same.

The AI and EI templates begin to drift further and further apart.

Think about that for a moment. It means that the way you've been taught you should be is not the way you were designed to be. And the bigger the gap between how you are 'designed' and how you have been 'created' the more difficulty you are likely to experience. It all creates *conflict* and conflict is the source of all emotional ills. Including depression. Conflict between how you *want* to be – a lot of which might be subconscious – and how you believe you *have* to be. The battle between nature and nurture has been raging for many a year – but nurture gets it wrong far more often than nature!

Now, the important thing is not to get involved in any sort of 'blame game' – those who brought you up were doing the best they could manage, given the resources they had to do the job with at the time. Like you, they could not control what they felt, only what they did with what they felt. They could only use what they themselves had been taught... and of course, they also were subject to the same conflicts as everybody else. In any case, you could blame them as much as you want but it wouldn't make any difference. It wouldn't improve your life. But what we're going to do here might well do just that. There's not room here to discuss every single possible problem, since that would take several books that were twice the size of this one! Instead, we're going to look at something much easier to grasp and work with – the outcome of personality clashes. Those who brought you up would have been behaving predominantly in one of the three main modes – Warrior, Settler or Nomad. We can safely ignore the secondary personality type because that would not make itself felt as must as the predominant one. There are quite a few possibilities of parent mixes:

- Warrior, Warrior
- Warrior, Nomad
- Warrior, Settler
- Nomad, Warrior
- Nomad, Nomad
- Nomad, Settler
- Settler, Settler

If we now add the possibility of each type of child to those combinations, you can probably work out that there are twenty-one possibilities – and that doesn't take account of positive or negative orientation, male or female! It's still enough to complete our task here though. The important thing to be aware of is that the conflict will quite often result in somebody trying to be a different type. We touched upon that subject in Chapter Six but we're looking deeper this time and also looking at how you can 'reset' at least part of that EI template.

The best situation is where the parents are different from each other and the child is the same as one of the parents. This at least allows a certain amount of identification and also recognition that not everybody is the same but neither is everybody different. We could investigate every single possibility here... but we won't. Instead we'll look at where depression might stem from and, later on, what to do with what you discover. It might not be the case that the depression comes entirely from these situations but it's extremely likely that it will have at least a part to play, even if the depression only became obvious when you were well into adulthood. (Working out how your parents *seemed to be as far as you were concerned* – Warrior, Nomad or Settler – will help you to make sense of the difficulties you might have encountered during your formative years.)

Most problems arise in the 'triangular' situation where the child is different from both parents. This probably makes sense straight away but just in case, it's because the child cannot identify completely with either parent and can also see that the parents are different from each other. In addition to this rather uncomfortable circumstance, neither parent can fully understand the needs and desires of the child. There are three of these combinations:

1. Warrior, Nomad parents, Settler child
2. Warrior and Settler parents, Nomad child
3. Nomad and Settler parents, Warrior child

The second most likely problematic situation is where the parents are the same as each other but the child is different – the mismatch:

4. Warrior and Warrior parents, Settler child
5. Warrior and Warrior parents, Nomad child
6. Nomad and Nomad parents, Warrior child
7. Nomad and Nomad parents, Settler child
8. Settler and Settler parents, Warrior child
9. Settler and Settler parents, Nomad child

We'll investigate enough of each for you to be able to understand exactly why problems can arise from them – and we're going to be looking at the situations which can easily trigger depression in later life. It's important to recognise that children are extraordinarily perceptive and aware of the parents' basic behaviour even if they couldn't name the types. It's also worth noting that each parent will attempt to mould the child in their own image – unless they know about the Warrior, Nomad and Settler concept of course. We're looking here at parental influence because even though there *are* other inputs, we tend to instinctively model ourselves on those who are bringing us up.

A side effect in every one of the situations that follow is the possibility of feeling like the 'odd one out' which, on its own can, create feelings of insecurity – it probably won't *cause* depression but it can be a contributory factor. What is certain is that it starts to widen the gap between what the child really wants to happen and what they have to put up with – in other words, the continual separation of the EI and AI templates.

The triangle

Warrior, Nomad – Settler child: This is potentially one of the worst-case scenarios. The Settler personality instinctively wants to be part of the tribe, yet recognises that the Warrior and Nomad don't share the same idea. The hard-wired instinctive drive to be an integral part of the group is, therefore, unfulfilled, fostering a subconscious idea of being unacceptable. In addition, the Settler child can be criticised by the Warrior for being 'soft' while the Nomad might insist on participation in situations which the Settler abhors.

Offsets: Where the Settler child receives plenty of affection and recognises they are definitely a valued part of the family (the tribe) the fact that they are different from either parent ceases to be of importance. In these circumstances, the Settler child can grow up to be a confident and caring individual who can make a great contribution to their environment.

Warrior, Settler – Nomad child: The worst thing about this situation is that the parents are likely to misread the child.

They might mistake enthusiasm for recklessness, optimism for stupidity and natural precocity for promiscuity. The child, in turn, recognises that one parent criticises anything they really want to do, the other one worries about it, and they both attempt to stifle the more exciting plans and ideas. It can eventually generate the subconscious idea that enjoyment of life comes at the price of disapproval by others.

Offsets: It is important to listen to the sometimes extravagant ideas of the Nomad child, sharing their enthusiasm before highlighting why it's not actually a *good* idea. They crave recognition and praise and can lose their inventive skills if they get too little of it. Allowing them to impress when it's deserved can result in an innovative and entrepreneurial adult who can achieve much.

Nomad, Settler – Warrior child: The mistake that parents can so easily make here is in seeking to control the forcefulness of their child – the problem is that neither of them have the instincts for it and the child will recognise it. The Nomad might be ineffectively dramatic, the Settler despairing, and the result can be either that the child acquires arrogance and believes they can get away with *anything*, or defiantly assumes a mantle of nastiness. The lessons of adult life can lead to anger... and depression at perceived lack of control in the world.

Offsets: Recognition that it's natural for this child to be hell-bent on having their own way, yet with a calmly implemented insistence on compromise when necessary, will help to develop self-control. Encouraging the assertive nature to be expressed politely and rationally with respect for the differing opinions of others can reap great benefits, and much success in life can be the result.

Two against one

Here, there is less need to look at the effects upon individual personality of the child than at what the combined force of parental personality might create. This is far greater than in the triangle situation, since the parents will appear to be, to the child, just one force so we'll look at the overall effect it might have on each child personality, in particular where the relationship is not particularly harmonious. There is a situation when the personality of the parents is the same as that of the child – and that can lead to some very fraught situations! In these cases, it's the suppression of natural instincts that creates that EI/AI conflict situation.

It should be obvious that only the vaguest of outlines are given here – a full study would need far more than just this book. But you'll still be able to see how problems arise and later, how to reclaim as much of the *real* you as possible.

Warrior, Warrior: Both parents are likely to be inclined towards control and criticism. They are almost certain to present a united front as far as the child is concerned and unless they recognise and accept the underlying personality of their child (rare) it is likely that damage will be done by strictness, excessive control, and lack of sufficient explicit affection – implied affection isn't enough.

- The **Warrior** child might harbour anger or resentment towards authority, an overtly rebellious nature being a likely outcome
- Sullen inward frustration or obnoxious outrageousness that alienates most people is the likely outcome for the **Nomad** child
- The **Settler** child will suffer low self-esteem as a result of not being able to be as 'tough' as parents indicated. Doormat syndrome is probable

Nomad, Nomad: This unstable partnership will seldom maintain any sense of continuity in the home or anywhere else. It's probable that there will be fairly frequent exhibitions of irresponsibility and/or over-the-top animosity about the state of the relationship, along with exaggerated claims concerning finances, infidelity, sexual habits and behaviour, spending, personal hygiene and more.

- The perceptive **Warrior** child will fear that one or both parents will leave and this can result in trust issues later on. Possessiveness is likely
- The **Nomad** child is likely to experience problems concerning any form of restraint or self-discipline. Honesty and integrity might be sparse
- Internalisation and resultant self-blame will make an insecure adult of the **Settler** child here. Low or non-existent self-esteem is likely

Settler, Settler: This relationship is likely to be weak, illustrating that all that can be done with the uncomfortable aspects of life is accept and adapt. Unpleasant people have to be given the benefit of the doubt and assertiveness is either frowned upon or feared. Authority and the law are to be obeyed unquestioningly and confrontation is best avoided.

- The Settler ethos is unpalatable to the **Warrior** child. Parental control is likely to be weak and this can create a self-centred and selfish adult
- The **Nomad** child will scoff at the parents' ineffectual efforts at restraint. Recklessness and a need for instant gratification is likely
- The **Settler** child will be perfectly comfortable with their upbringing but may lack the ability to control their life. 'Doormat syndrome' is likely

Now what?

It's likely that you've recognised, somewhere in the above, your own parental background. Sometimes, the situation can lead directly to depression, while at other times it would instead create a 'time bomb' where the depression set in much later, when life just wasn't working as you believed it should... or perhaps as you had learnt it would. It doesn't much matter if you don't really identify with the likely outcomes shown for the child of your particular parental setup – all that is necessary is for you to understand that you weren't allowed to develop into the you that you were designed to be. Remember, though, that this is not a blame-laying exercise – those who brought you up did the best they could with the resources they had available to them at the time. *Yes, you have read that before (or something very like it) but it deserves repeating!* If you start laying blame all over the place, it will turn to resentment when you can't do anything about it... and all the time you could have been getting better instead.

So we can now set about the business of closing the gap between the EI and AI templates – you can never completely close it, due to the fact that we live in a society where we have to conform to certain ideals and rules. But you can close the gap to the point where it becomes tolerable. Fortunately, we don't need to analyse every single aspect of your life – that would take far too long! You've actually already started the process we need to work with, assuming that you've been doing the VMI exercises from Chapter Six, that is.

A tiny bit of easy preparation work is needed now; you need the three-word description of your basic self that you established in Chapter Six – for instance, *Determined, Optimistic, Intuitive* – along with whatever it was that revealed the 'essence' of your major VMI. Rearrange the order of the description so that the dominant attribute is first and write them down. For instance, if you are Settler with a secondary Warrior with the above descriptors, you would write: *Intuitive, Determined, Optimistic.*

Now add the artefact that carried the 'essence' of your dominant Part, so if your Settler VMI was typified by a bricklayer's trowel, book or a hat, for example, write that down after the three-word description.

Take a moment to create a VMI in your mind of that description. It might be different from any of the other three because we're embodying all traits in one image, but that's absolutely fine. With your eyes closed, play around with the image for a little while until it feels not just 'right' but also comfortable, as if it somehow seems to suit you perfectly. It might be a single image or it might be like an animation, cycling through three different images; it might even be a composite of three but when you're comfortable with what you have, it's right. Be sure to include the defining artefact (this maintains the focus on your dominant trait) and take all the time you need. This is an important exercise so keep at it until the image is as real as you can get it.

Got that? Good!

Now, remember that you have created this image in your own mind, based on your own imagination and your own thoughts. It is an honest representation of *you* in the way you see yourself and it's important that you resist any urges to change it after the next bit of work... So if you think you might want to change something, do it now!

The presentation

All right – now we're into the final part of this chapter. Holding the image in your mind imagine presenting yourself to whoever had the most input into your upbringing – this is usually parents of course, but not necessarily so. We want the person or people who had the most influence over you. When you have that idea clearly in your mind, imagine the sort of response you might get from them – if it's favourable, then your mind now knows that you have the approval of those who have been most influential upon you. Your work is done for this chapter and there's no real need to read any more of it (though you can if you want to, of course.)

Now, some people cannot bear to even start the process, feeling 'silly', sad, angry, daft, humiliated or some other negative response as soon as they try the exercise. If this is how it is for you, *that's what* **they** *gave you!* Somehow, they've conveyed repeatedly that you are foolish, dim, slow or whatever – even if you don't really remember actual occasions – and because they are the 'elders of the tribe', *you believed they were right.* There's no doubt about this, in case you're wondering. If you had created a totally different image, you would still have felt the same. If you presented as exactly like the same-sex individual in their relationship, you would *still* find those negative feelings. You don't deserve that, of course, and you deserve to be free from it. Later, there's a simple exercise that will help you to do just that.

If you were at ease with the idea only to discover that you found yourself imagining a response that was disapproving or in some other way negative, it tells you nothing other than that those who brought you up are incapable of understanding or accepting anything or anybody that is in any way different from them. They have small minds (not their fault) and cannot conceive of their own short-sightedness, or that their ideas are no more valid than those they mock. You can almost certainly recall times when they've mocked others for no good reason... other than their own anxiety about encountering 'stuff' that is different from the way they themselves are.

At best, they simply didn't understand you – *their problem.* At worst, they wanted to disempower you – again, their problem.

Repair work

Time to do a bit of restoration now... First of all, here's another question for you: If you had to choose, would you rather be giving it or getting it? Before you answer, consider the fact that they're handing out hurt to others, not just you, because of their own damage in their psyche. You, on the other hand, have a chance to repair most, if not all, the psychological injury that's occurred. So, which would you choose – to be like them or be the way you are seeking to be? If this book has done its work properly you will have chosen the latter. If not... well, it's difficult to see why you're still reading it!

Now for the last-but-one task in this chapter. You'll need to close your eyes for the first part of this one, so read it through first. You're going to do a presentation of that composite self again, the one with the artefact that represents your major trait. This time you will imagine presenting yourself to each of the VMIs singly, then to all three of them at once. Almost certainly, you will find approval from each and also from the entire group, and you can in that case rest assured that you are coming to terms with the way you really are.

Got that? Good – do it now... and before moving on to the last bit.

Right, the last task for this chapter, an easy one... write a description of the real you, starting with the three-word description that you created earlier. Now follow that with areas in everyday life where you would be using those leading traits, *Intuitive, Determined, Optimistic*, for instance. You can choose to write about a typical day in your life, or you can create an imaginary one as long as you keep it plausible and possible – and positive. You don't need to write a book – around two-hundred-and-fifty words will be enough. When you've done that, go back to the descriptions in Chapter Six and choose one of the negative traits from each type, making sure that they are things you've shown at times in the past. For instance, if you are Settler/Warrior, you might have: *Weak, Critical, Dramatic* or: *Moody, Blunt, Unreliable*.

Now read through that typical day, taking note of where any of those negative traits might have got in the way or otherwise spoilt things – there's no need to write it down, just notice how they tend to lead you back into depression. So, the moral of the story is: *practise using the positive attributes!* That and the VMI exercise you learnt in Chapter Six, or at least conjuring up each VMI in your mind on a daily basis, will strengthen everything else you are working at.

In the next chapter, we're going to be having a look at exactly why things might not always have turned out as you wanted them to, in spite of your best efforts – and what you can do about that. It's all to do with the four stages of learning...

Old Lessons Revisited

An Englishman abroad

The lessons of life are hard enough to learn but the biggest problem is that they are so often conducted by inept teachers! It's not their fault, mind, because they only learnt to be a parent by being a child and they can only teach later on what they've learnt themselves. And there's another problem, too. When what they are teaching doesn't produce the result they want, they assume not that there's something wrong with the lesson but with the student – and never mind that *they* couldn't make the lessons work either!

So they do the equivalent of the Englishman abroad... If what you're saying appears not to be understood, shout. And if it still doesn't get the right result, shout louder still. That's another thing they were taught. The problem with all this volume is that if the child remonstrates they are usually left in no doubt at all that it's never a good idea to challenge authority. The alternative, though, isn't much better and might well be worse – the child assumes, because they are told, that they are a waste of space, a useless article, a hopeless case, dim, daft or just plain stupid.

We don't physically remember those lessons, perhaps, after we've grown up, though we still act upon them subconsciously. But that's about to change...

Chapter Nine

The four stages of learning

You've probably not thought in a great deal of detail about the learning process. Most people haven't. Yet once you recognise how it actually works, you begin to discover that you can improve it no end. You are also able to be a bit easier on yourself about things that you don't seem to get right – and whatever you might have been told or believe, it's never because you're dim! There are four specific stages involved in learning *anything* and they are:

1. **Unconscious Incompetence** – in this state, you don't know what it is you don't know and you're blissfully unaware of your lack of knowledge
2. **Conscious Incompetence** – here, you've discovered there's something you don't know how to do
3. **Conscious Competence** – now you've done a bit of learning and you can do what it is you need to do... But you have to think about it
4. **Unconscious Competence** – at last you've mastered a skill and you can do it without thought... it's become almost a part of you

A little bit more explanation will clarify things a bit more just to be on the safe side. So here's a simple explanation: if an individual had never seen a bicycle, they wouldn't know such a thing existed or what it was supposed to do. That's *unconscious incompetence*. Then they discover bicycles and at about the same time discover they don't know how to ride it and they keep on falling off. That's *conscious incompetence*. After some time and practice, they are able to maintain their balance... as long as they think about it and concentrate on keeping the machine upright. That's *conscious competence*. Finally, after a lot more practice, riding a bicycle becomes an automatic process. *Unconscious competence* has now been achieved and there's no need to think about what they're doing in order to do it properly.

There are many other examples. Learning a song you didn't know existed and eventually being able to sing it all the way through without thinking; learning a new recipe for a dish of some sort; learning a dance routine... You can probably think of a lot more now you've been introduced to the idea. But you might still be wondering what on earth this has got to do with you and depression. The answer might surprise you – depression is something you've learnt to do without thinking. You are *unconsciously competent* at depression!

But that might not be the whole story because it's highly possible that the depression is reinforced by quite a few things at which you are *consciously incompetent* – things you know that you don't know how to do properly, if at all, but believe you should. Many people with depression have a whole catalogue of those, most often associated with such things as:

- Relationships
- Social situations
- Dealing with 'awkward' people
- Sexual matters
- Money management
- Housework
- Self-worth

There are more, of course, but those listed are very common. But now let's consider something... that word 'should'. It is a fact that if you 'should' be able to do something then you *would* be able to do it. If you can't, and yet it's within the bounds of physical and mental possibility for you, then you are lacking part of the knowledge that is needed. You're not yet at the stage of *conscious competence,* so it's a fact that you **should not** be able to do it, because you don't have all the resources necessary. Not your fault. There's a saying that's worth remembering: *if the student cannot do then the teacher has not taught.*

So taking any one of those situations listed (or anything else that's more relevant) ask yourself how you discovered: (a) what you were supposed to be able to do; and (b) how you know that what you discovered was right. Also, was the person or people who taught you competent themselves? And if so, how did they pass the knowledge on to you? Perhaps surprisingly, the most likely answer here is that you were never actually taught whatever you've selected to investigate. But when somebody wants to learn how to ride a bike, they need somebody else to hold the machine upright so they can get the feeling of what they're 'supposed' to do. It's vaguely possible that they might eventually learn without help just by continual experimentation but much more likely that they would give up, deciding they were in some way inferior to those who could already do it. And this is very important: *All the time they believed they couldn't do it they never would be able to. But if somebody held the back of the saddle for them, they would soon get the hang of it.*

Life is exactly like that. If you believe you can't do something, you probably never will. But if you believe, instead, that you've not been shown properly how to do whatever it is you want to do, you will take steps to find out what it is you're lacking. You will seek to move forward from that state of *conscious incompetence* and you know what? When you become *consciously competent* instead you will feel like a champion! And when you get to the next stage, it will all seem so normal to you that you will begin to believe that there never was a real problem in the first place. It is a fact that what you can think of as standard 'life skills' can be taught, and if they can be taught, they can be learnt. By you. But there might be another problem to overcome first.

First impressions last

The most effective lesson you've been given, the one you've really taken on board, is that you are in some way a lost cause. Maybe you learnt that you're dim, lazy, stupid, thick, retarded, incapable, substandard, not like your sibling(s), not like your father, not like the rest of the family... or maybe you were just taught that you are in some way inferior to other beings. And if you've been subjected to such lessons (which you might not actually remember) so early on in life that they were part of the first impressions you had about what people thought of you, they have almost certainly become an entrenched part of who you believe you are. They might not have been given in words; they can just easily be conveyed by a roll of the eyes, a shake of the head, laughter, a muttered *'for goodness sake'*, or just a look. And if you didn't actually receive those lessons, then you're self-taught! But that would only mean that someone prepared the way for you to readily arrive at such a negative view of self.

We've already done a bit of work on this sort of thing, of course, and now we're going to do a little more. Without giving it a lot of thought, describe yourself in a single word or a short phrase. Write it down. Underneath it, write down how you discovered that. *"I just know,"* is not an acceptable answer, nor is writing down the *results* of what you've described yourself as – the things that have happened *because of it*. For instance, *"I do stupid things,"* is not a good answer. *"Somebody told me,"* is valid, as long as you can remember who the 'somebody' was. *"I found out I'd been doing something completely wrong,"* is not a correct answer – that just shows you hadn't been taught the right way to do whatever it was. *"I heard somebody talking about me,"* is valid but once again, only if you can remember who it was. There are three possibilities:

1. You can remember distinctly how you discovered this 'truth'

2. You haven't been able to define how you discovered it – it's just a belief

3. You've realised that how you described yourself is not actually accurate

We'll have a look at each of those situations separately. First, number 1 – **you remember distinctly how you discovered this truth.** Well, the only valid answer is that somebody told you or you heard somebody talking about you. Anything else would be an assessment based on something you do or don't do... but what you do or don't do is based on what you believe you discovered about self.

Now here's something very important which you will read more about later on. The physical brain doesn't understand, know, or care if something is 'good' or 'bad' – it makes no judgement at all. It's no more selective than a typewriter keyboard. Whatever key is pressed will create a letter on the screen or paper whether that was what you really wanted or not. All it does, in fact, is monitor the continual stream of information it receives, some from the outside world, some from your body, some even from your thoughts. It tests to see if there's an existing pattern of behaviour (which includes more thoughts) associated with that information. If there is, and there's been no information to counteract it, it will do the same thing again – and as unbelievable as it might seem, all this happens before you know about it! Even if you decide to change your mind that decision is made before you are aware of it, because the speedy part of the brain has found a different behaviour to activate.

This is why it's so difficult to break a habit or to change the way you do things once they've reached that *unconscious competence* level of learning. The pattern in the brain exists and it operates without any input from you. Now, some of those patterns are obvious, things like tying shoelaces or using a knife and fork – you know you're doing them because there's a sound reason to do them. But the brain is very subtle sometimes, creating a *feeling* for no reason other than that it's detected a pattern where that feeling has always been created. All you are aware of is – feeling depressed.

Later on you will read more about this rather strange process and how we might use it beneficially but right now it's only necessary for you to recognise that if you're to get better, you need to make some changes to the way your brain is doing things! You need to make a change to one of the *unconsciously competent* behaviours. Fortunately, this is easier than you might think, because the brain responds to *everything*. Let's come back to what you wrote down about yourself for a moment or two. If you can remember somebody telling you about it, or hearing somebody talking about it, then that's part of what the brain is operating on, in response to the input from the world. So now we're going to interfere with that process to at least weaken it, if we can't stop it in its tracks.

Challenge what you heard. **Really** *challenge it. All you heard was another person's ideas, something that another person thought. And what does it say about them if they* **intended** *it to harm you? Will you give credibility to someone who works like that? And what if you heard it being said to somebody else? It's still only somebody else's thoughts, somebody who talks about others behind their backs. Wonder why they said it by all means, but assume now that they had some reason for saying it, something their brain was doing, that you know nothing about.* **Challenge it!**

It might be the case that you've heard it several times from different people but that would only mean you believe what you *think* they meant... and there's an important saying about that: *"I know you believe what you think I said but I'm not sure you realise that what you heard is not what I meant."* That little saying sums up the basis of all sorts of misunderstandings.

Let's pretend something for a moment or two. Let's pretend there's some element of truth in what you heard. Perhaps you *are* a bit daft, selfish, self-centred or whatever... but did you choose it? Do you set out to be it? Does it mean you should suffer because of it? Does it really matter? *It does not!* There are many slightly daft, occasionally selfish and self-centred individuals 'out there' who are loved by their friends, accept that most people are nothing special, and have a perfectly 'normal' life. Whatever you might have thought in the past, there's no price for not being 'amazing'.

Challenge what you've believed about yourself up until now. Decide what you'll choose to believe instead. That'll be enough to weaken that *unconscious competence* in self-doubt that your brain has been operating on!

Just a belief

The next possibility is that you couldn't define how you discovered what you've always believed about yourself. It's just a belief and it's almost certain that you're comparing how you *feel* with how others *look*, just as you read in Chapter Two. It's like comparing a spoon with angry – it's just not a valid comparison because they are entirely different concepts and you cannot ever assess what somebody feels like by studying their appearance. So forget what you think about them and work out what you really think about yourself. Do you *really* feel that way or are you just frightened that's how others might see you?

While growing up, we are told not to think too much of ourselves, and that can lead to a feeling that if you think anything even *vaguely* complimentary to yourself, this is necessarily a Bad Thing and no good at all will come of it. It's a situation that can so easily lead to you half-believing, or fearing, that others will see you in a poor light – and of course, you will imagine the thing that feels worst to you and then fear that this is exactly how you are seen.

So now spend a few moments putting into actual lucid thoughts – writing them down is a good idea – the ideas about how you fear others see you. Then do the same thing with how *you* see *them*. Now give each set of thoughts a 'reality rating' on a scale of 1—10 to assess how true-to-life you really believe those thoughts are. Can they *really* see what you think or fear they can, even if it were true? Do you really believe they are that perceptive? Do you really think they even care? Most people don't, actually, and will tend to see what they already believe is there – and that's nothing to do with you but is a reflection of their own life, as you read earlier. Do you know *for sure* that how you see them is truly the way they are and that they're not just good at projecting an image? Do you believe everybody shows their true self to the entire world, or might they be indulging in a bit of salesmanship, presenting themselves in what they imagine is a good light?

It's odds on that those 1—10 scores are rather lower than you thought in the first place!

Realisation

The third possibility is that you've now come to the conclusion that the way you've tended to see yourself isn't entirely accurate. Might not even be more than 'a little accurate' in fact. If that should be the case, then you're making great headway and what you were thinking about yourself until this realisation was the result of nothing more than **habit.** Funny things, habits, especially destructive ones. They can linger for years yet depart in an instant, especially when you've been reading a book about them, like this one.

Now, whichever of those three categories you found yourself in, go back and cross out (not erase) that short description of self and write a different word or short phrase instead – and do be sure to make it something that you would love to know that others realised about you. Keep it realistic and make certain it's something you truly know and belief about your self...

It's highly probable that what you have chosen as a 'new and improved' description of self belongs to your major personality trait... but if that seems not to be the case it might indicate that you have more affinity with the part of you that it *does* belong to. Often, in this situation, the new description appears to be associated with the Warrior part of self, and where this is not the major trait it simply shows a subconscious recognition of the strength of that part. It doesn't mean necessarily that your assessment was wrong, only that when it comes down to it, you prefer to see within you the strength of the Warrior. Of course, you might instead discover that you identify with the adapt-ability and intuition of the Settler or the enthusiasm and energy of the Nomad. Whatever you chose, you're now going to strengthen it!

It's an eyes-closed job so read the exercise first before you try it. First, do the 'breathing thing' to find the quiet moment of now, then think of each VMI in turn, the Warrior, Nomad and Settler (it doesn't matter which order) vividly imagining each one illus-trating that new description of self in turn. Whatever it is, the Warrior will show it in a grounded fashion, the Nomad will be proud of it, and the Settler will be quietly pleased that they can access this positive attitude when they need it. Run it like a video clip in your mind half-a-dozen times or so.

If you get it right, it will get easier with each run through and by the time you get to the last one, it should have ceased to seem remarkable. If this hasn't happened, run it some more until it does!

Got that? Good... ***Do it now!***

When that little exercise has been completed successfully, you will have achieved *conscious competence* with seeing yourself in a new light; and after a while, especially if you practise the exercise a few times, you will move into that wonderful state of *unconscious competence* as far as self-image is concerned. Then you're **really** getting somewhere.

We'll finish this chapter with a little test to see how you're getting on at a subconscious level. You remember the safe with the combination lock in which you hid that 'secret' in Chapter Five? Can you remember the Combination number? If you can't – excellent. It means that your subconscious simply can't be bothered with it any more. If you *can* remember the combination, then in your mind, open the safe and take out the photograph you hid in there. Now, assume that it had a score of '10' on a level of discomfort when you placed it in there in the beginning and now reassess it. Be honest. It's likely that it's lower and that's a good sign which you probably don't need explained. Either way, put it back in the safe and spin that lock again to keep it safe. You can come back to it another time...

In the next chapter, you'll be working very directly with the part of you that knows – perhaps *knew* – how to feel depressed and teaching it a thing or two!

Chapter Ten

Plausible, possible and fair

In Chapter Five, we touched upon the difficulties associated with the idea of positive thinking and how it's actually far more natural to think negatively. As you've already seen though, it's not sufficient to just wallow about in your naturally-occurring negative thoughts and expect life to turn out the way you always wanted – you need to work out what to do about the pitfalls if they occur. Then, though, we were talking about dealing with the difficulties that life throws at all of us from time to time, but now we're going to look at how to get what you want out of life. And that's a completely different kettle of fish!

The most important thing of all to remember is that all the positive thinking in the world won't get you stuff. You can read any number of websites and books about the 'amazing' phenomena of the law of attraction; they will tell you how you only have to know exactly what you want, why you want it, and believe that you deserve it and it will somehow come tumbling into your lap.

Bunkum.

There are those who swear it works and will tell you endless tales that are supposed to prove the point about how attraction works... but the examples they give don't stand up to any tests. A favourite one goes something like this: *"I decided I wanted to buy a red Mazda sports car; visualised it and dreamt about it and the next thing I knew I saw red Mazda sports cars wherever I went!"* Well, that's probably true but they would have been there anyway, just not noticed until the brain and mind were focussed on them. Either that or a whole lot of owners of red Mazda sports cars wondered why and how they ended up miles from where they wanted to be... And what about the 'amazing phenomena of manifestation'? You probably know that one: all you have to do is desperately want something, truly believe you'll get it, and it will suddenly be there for you. There's a flaw here, though, in that if more and more people start manifesting what they want, who's going to manufacture all that stuff? And who's going to pay for it?

And the point is...

You might now be wondering what on earth all this has to do with depression. Well, on its own, it doesn't have any connection at all unless part of what makes you feel bad is that you can't seem to get what you want and at the same time believe that almost everybody else can. But the point is that it illustrates a vital fact:

*If you want something, you have to **do** something.*

It doesn't matter if you're after some material thing or an emotional state; that rule still holds. And even more important are the two rules that some people overlook and others don't even know exist:

- Whatever you want must be plausible, possible and fair
- Whatever you seek must be for *you* and you alone, not for anybody else

That first one is in many ways the most important because everything you want to achieve *must* pass the 'PPF' test. If it doesn't, it's almost certainly doomed to failure. **Plausible** means that the goal is definitely achievable. Wanting to feel enthusiastic and to enjoy being alive is plausible. Wanting that to happen tomorrow after being depressed for years is definitely not – time to create change is needed. **Possible** is more to do with your own capabilities and needs the *degree* of possibility to be taken into account. So wanting to earn more money is possible, while wanting to become the richest person in the world is less so. **Fair...** Now there's a whole can of worms. This really crosses over into that second rule; that whatever you seek must be for you and you alone. If you're trying to get your own back on somebody who's hurt you in some way 'to see how they like it', you will end up doing yourself more harm. There's no mystery about this, nothing spiritual or magical – it's just the fact that your brain can only hold one type of idea at a time. And because the human animal is egocentric, your subconscious/brain will believe that whatever you have in your thoughts is intended for you to find.

It doesn't matter that you consciously know that you want to heap trial and tribulation on *somebody else's* head, your brain will still do everything it can to bring it upon you – and it will succeed unless you're very lucky! This is because the brain is not in the least discriminatory as you have already read; It bears repeating: the brain neither knows nor cares whether something is 'good' or 'bad' (in fact, it has no notion that those concepts even exist.) All it deals with is data and because it is *your* brain it will focus that data on *your* world, rather than anybody else's. If that data is about mayhem, it will seek mayhem around you. If it is about energy and enthusiasm, then it will seek energy and enthusiasm *around you*. And it is a fact that the more you believe it, the more vividly you can imagine it; the more likely it is that you will find ideas that will lead you towards it. So the **PPF** test must be applied to any plan, any idea you might have, to help you get what you want out of life.

There is something to be aware of here... you might well be thinking about what you want but if at the same time you're fearing that you will get something else instead, be careful! **Fear** is one of the two most powerful motivators known to man (the other one is **greed**) and because it's stronger your brain is more inclined to act upon it. It will actually begin to generate ideas designed to lead you toward that which you fear! If you discover fear anywhere in your plans for yourself, either find a way to dispel the fear or choose a different plan.

Now for the second point, what you want must be for you and you alone. This is not actually as easy as it sounds to implement, purely because many of us are brought up to believe that 'selfishness' is a Bad Thing and that putting others before ourselves is a Good Thing. But there's something very odd about some of this because we're also taught that we have to learn to look after ourselves and that not doing so is somehow a sign of weakness. And then there's that thing where we are told we shouldn't let people take advantage of us. So, in effect, that means we have to look after ourselves by putting others first and while we're putting them first we shouldn't let them take advantage of us. A bit of a tall order, that.

So when it comes to deciding what you want, you can cheerfully forget about all that selfishness nonsense and decide what you actually want for yourself. Not to make a partner feel better or happier. Not to convince anybody that you can now fend for yourself. Not so that people who've helped you or cared for you can bask in a nice warm glow of satisfaction at the wonderful thing they've done.

Let's put this in a rather neat nutshell: *If you want to feel better than you do, decide how **you** want to feel and forget all about what anybody else will think or say, or what they would advise.* If it's purely for you and it passes that 'PPF' test, it has the highest chance of success – and you're going to be doing some more work shortly which is designed to take you ever closer to feeling the way you want to feel.

Now there's just one more thing to take care of before moving into this next exercise, and that is to ensure that you know exactly what you want to feel. "Happy' is not really a good answer because it never lasts very long. That might not make a lot of sense until you realise that whatever is making you happy either goes away or becomes 'normal' after a while, then you're back to square one. 'Better' doesn't work, either, for pretty much the same reasons, plus the fact that 'better' is not a feeling at all but just a statement of comparison.

Here's a list of suitable answers but you can choose something else if you don't like any of them:

- Self-confident
- Energetic
- Optimistic
- Light-hearted
- Worthwhile
- Equal to others
- Cope with living

Choose carefully, because the exercise you will be doing will be much more difficult, perhaps even impossible, if what you have chosen is not for you and you alone but is partly for somebody else. It's fine if somebody else will benefit – for instance, you becoming energetic improves their life in some way – as long as you didn't choose it for that purpose over something else that you would really have preferred. Be selfish!

Parts apart

The exercise that follows takes up the rest of this chapter – and is one of the most important exercises in the whole book. This one is to be done 'as you go' rather than reading it through first (it works far more effectively that way) so let's get started with no further ado!

You might find a tendency to want to shy away from some of what follows here but that's all completely normal when you're in the process of making major changes. It's all about survival... and the subconscious will tend to try to avoid change because if what you've been doing has led to you surviving – and it has, because you're still here – it will seek to do more of the same. This is exactly the reason why making change is so difficult; the subconscious has to learn that what is being introduced is at least as good a survival package as the one that's currently running. Well, you've done all right so far because you've got to this part of the book! So now we're going to enhance the change you've already started making.

You've already done some work similar to this exercise when you created the VMIs of your Warrior, Nomad and Settler parts of self. This time, though, you're going to be creating an image – well, two, actually – for quite a different reason which will soon become obvious. *It's important that you do this one as you go if you're to get the best out of it. Reading it through first is likely to weaken it, so work as if the book were a therapist taking you through a session.* You really need to be in a quiet place and on your own if possible, so, if that's not really convenient at the moment for any reason at all, it would be best to leave it now and come back when you are able.

All right, now you're ready to start. This is a 'lite' version of 'Parts Therapy' which is used all over the world to help people deal with all sorts of difficulties, and used well it can be a powerful method of creating change. To begin, create an image in your mind of what the depressed Part of you would look like if it were real. It might just look like a version of you, or it could be something entirely different and not necessarily even human. Although this is best done with an image in your mind's eye, as with other areas in this book you can use just thoughts if you find visualisation difficult. You can do the exercise with your eyes open or closed but be sure you've created as vivid an image as possible before continuing. Be aware of colours, sounds, smells, touch, age and so on, exactly as when you were creating the VMIs in Chapter Six, though this part doesn't need a name unless you feel the need to give it one. If creating this image feels uncomfortable *do **not** turn away from it or try to banish it!* Instead, just hold it in your mind until the uncomfortable feeling subsides – and it will.

When you feel comfortable with holding this image in your

mind you can move on to the next step, which might possibly prove a little more difficult. *Only* difficult though and you'll just need to persevere a little to complete it. This time, you're going to create an image of the Part of you that embodies the feeling you chose earlier, whether it was from that list or just something that occurred to you without really thinking too hard about it. Now, if you've suddenly felt a wave of doubt or apprehension, that *could* be an indicator that you have not chosen as wisely as you might have done. So check:

- Do you *truly* want to feel that way?
- Is that goal *exactly* what you want for *you?*

If the answer to either of those questions is 'No', then choose again and think carefully! On the other hand if the answer to both those questions is 'Yes' then just accept that some trepidation is completely normal – after all, you're moving into uncharted territory as far as you're concerned. This can help: think about how your life will be when you actually do feel like that. Not 'if' but 'when'. And don't just decide it will be 'great' or 'wonderful' – be specific. Name some of the things you'll be able to do that you can't do yet. Name some of the things that you'll be able to stop doing – which might include negative thinking and catastrophising. And if that makes you even more uncomfortable, *go back and choose again being even more careful this time!* It's essential that you're keen and eager to get this process underway, otherwise you'll spend a lot of time tripping over your own feet instead of making headway...

Okay. You've now got the idea in mind and you're happy enough with it to begin to imagine that Part, in exactly the same way as you did the depressed Part. Because this sort of positive feeling is probably less familiar to you, you might need to have a couple of 'takes' at it... You can redo it as many times as you like, in fact, and the only important thing is to just keep going until you are pleased with the image you have created and actually *want* to feel and be like that. Then you're ready to move on to the actual work of this exercise which, although it might feel rather odd at first, is a very powerful way of getting to some 'secret' truths.

This part is best done with your eyes closed and in that special quiet moment of 'Now' (which you can use the 'breathing thing' to find if you wish) so read the section in italics, complete it to the best of your ability, then open your eyes again to move on to the section that follows.

Find the quiet place in your thoughts then bring the depressed Part into your mind, making it vivid enough that you can see it clearly in your mind's eye (or thoughts.) Now we come to the 'meat' of this exercise, the part that might feel distinctly 'odd' at first. You're going to ask Depressed Part a question out loud – which is why you need to be on your own, of course! Here's the question:

"What is it that you try to do for me?"

You are unlikely to hear words but you'll get a feeling or a thought after a little while. Then you ask another question:

"Why do you find the need to do that?"

Again, you won't hear words but you will find an answer in your mind if you wait for a while. Then, whatever the answer, continue with:

"Okay, thank you for that. But you don't have to do that any more because things are different now... So you can rest now. Is that okay?"

If you get a 'No' answer, then you'll need to explore more but this is actually very rare. When all seems well, you can say:

"Thank you. I'm going to introduce you to somebody, so don't go away."

It's important that you complete the above exercise before moving on and you might already have worked out that you're going to introduce the other Part you created. To make description easy, we'll assume it's 'Worthwhile Part' though of course you'll use whatever you created. Again, you'll have your eyes closed, so read the passage in italics first, as before, then continue.

Find the quiet place and bring Worthwhile Part into your mind, making it as vivid as possible. Thank him/her/it for being there and ask this question:

"Are you ready to help me start my new life?"

Wait for the answer, which should be a 'Yes' if you've prepared properly. If not, investigate by asking questions to find out what needs to happen – the answers will appear in your thoughts and it's important that you accept them! When all is well, introduce Worthwhile Part to Depressed Part (using whatever words work for you) and ask Worthwhile Part to promise Depressed Part that he/she/it will look after you and protect you every bit as carefully as Depressed Part has done over the years until now. See them shake hands as if a contract has been agreed, then watch as Depressed Part leaves, gradually fading into the distance, finally to disappear. Then thank Worthwhile Part for their help and open your eyes when you're ready to do so.

Now, that might have all seemed very odd but it's actually a version of a style of therapy that's carried out in therapists' offices across the world every day. And all you have to do to keep it active and strong is, when something doesn't work the way you wanted it to, momentarily think of Worthwhile Part (or whatever you selected, Optimistic Part, Energetic Part, Equal to Others Part, Light-Hearted Part, etc.) and think of how that Part will deal with the situation.

It's simple – but it works!

Moving On

Near the end of the beginning

Well we're really getting into the plan now! It's highly likely that you're already feeling quite a lot better about yourself and your future but don't worry if you're not where you want to be yet. We've still got work to do. And just as in films, races, exams and all sorts of preparation work, the most energetic and exciting bit happens towards the end. At the moment, you're still partly in touch with the threads and restrictions of life that you've been dogged by for so long... But the preparation has put everything in place for you to finally break free!

There's something very important that you have to do first though, and that is to accept once and for all that you will give up the idea of using your depression to get you 'off the hook', get you out of doing things, or to try to get attention... which doesn't make you feel any better anyway. If you want to get attention, do it the right way – be impressive!

Chapter Eleven

Cutting yourself free

When something goes disastrously wrong, it's sometimes referred to these days as 'a car crash'. And when you suffer from depression, it's easy to feel that this describes your whole life... Well, if this was you at the beginning of the book it probably isn't now (unless you've just happened to turn to this page to see if it's any good!) But even if there are a few remnants of the feeling, you are about to cut yourself completely free at last and get the best life you could ever have – and a lot of it will be precisely *because* of the way things were originally.

We'll have a look at two extremes. There are those people who grew up in a nice house in a nice street in a nice area, with a nice family. Who went to a nice school then got a nice job in a nice firm with a nice pay packet every month... And yet still ended up with depression. It happens far more frequently than you might have imagined and it's at least as difficult to deal with as if there was a valid reason for the depression in the first place. At the other end of the scale is the individual who grew up in a deprived area with what can best be described as a 'lumpy' childhood in a shabby street, with an indifferent family and inadequate teachers, as a result of which they ended up in a dead-end job with poor wages... and depression.

If your life has been closer to that second example than the first, then you have a distinct advantage over those apparently fortunate individuals born into comparative luxury and well-being. This is because relatively small changes can make relatively big differences, so that the information and exercises in this book – and we haven't finished yet – can provide the help and encouragement needed to create and maintain positive change. And if at some point later on you feel yourself 'sagging' (unlikely, actually) you already have the experience of getting yourself out of the mire – and how good it feels when you do – and will automatically make moves to pick yourself up again. Well, unless you actually wanted the depression to get a grip of you again… but then we've covered that in some detail at the beginning of the book!

If, however, you were a privileged child (though you might not recognise it) then your problem is very specific. You're still a slave to the inheritance of your ancient ancestors but there is a huge difference. They had a goal to pursue; you probably don't. Not at the moment, anyway… And that's where problems often start. The human animal never did find sustained happiness, even contentment, from possessions or the way things are; they too rapidly become 'normal' and so we start to aspire to something more.

The man who has a bike wants a small car; the one with a small car wants a bigger car; once he has the bigger car he wants the big house to go with it, perhaps some land, maybe a boat… and so on.

The one whose life is humdrum wants excitement; the one whose life is hectic wants a calm haven; when she finds the calm haven, she wants to share it with someone… But when she shares it with someone it soon becomes 'normal' and life become humdrum…

What we're saying in a rather long-winded manner is that you need to be chasing something. If you have no purpose in life, no goal, it's extraordinarily difficult to feel that there is any point to your life – and that's the route to depression! Not only that, but if you grew up in that privileged manner and you have already been used to having the things that others so avidly pursue, boredom can soon set in… And it is so easy to confuse boredom and depression, a concept that was covered at the beginning of the book. But you're still here, so we have to assume that it's depression in your case. So here's the most important part of the 'prescription' to get you better: if you've only been reading the book (which is actually very likely) start to *do* something about what you're reading! Any or all of the exercises will help. But you need one thing more in your case, and that is something to pursue. 'Happiness' isn't a goal but a response, so that doesn't count – you need something you can't just buy or obtain in some way. Something that requires some effort on your part. It doesn't really matter what, and it can be anything from learning how to grow prize-winning vegetables to becoming an airline captain; from learning to play the sitar (one of the most difficult musical instruments in the world to learn) to trekking into the depths of Mongolia or Tibet.

Freedom

Whether you grew up in a slum or a mansion, one rule remains the same: *you need to let go of what you currently perceive to be part of your identity*. Unless, that is, you have already 'done a number' in that particular department. But it's odds on that your self-image still has a good part of what it always had, still carries the threads of your views about the way you fit into the world *with* the depression instead of without it. So take a few moments now to do a simple exercise 'on the fly' – it doesn't actually need any preparation. Let your mind drift back to some time when you have been particularly aware of depression and imagine how you see yourself in that memory. Make it fairly vivid – what you might be wearing, the expression on your face, the way you're moving or sitting, and so on. Does it feel familiar? It probably does – after all, you've had a lot of practice at this! Now change anything about that impression and ideally be outrageously different from the way you really are. Change your hairstyle, the type of clothes you're wearing, the way you're moving, sitting or standing. If you're female, be flirty and precocious if you like; if you're male, perhaps be roguish and 'bad'. Notice how it feels as you allow the flight of fancy to play itself through. What would happen if you really *did* behave like that at the time you are thinking of? Supposing you behaved just like that the next time you were in a similar situation? What would happen then? Play the scene all the way through in your mind until it 'runs out of steam' – *but be sure to avoid catastrophising!*

Now, if what you were imagining was negatively orientated, go back and go through it all again, looking for the positive aspects (they are always there somewhere!) remembering nobody is suggesting that you actually do these things – it's simply a game of imagination. When you've found the positive angle, even if it's just that you didn't have to be answerable to anybody else, or that nobody was controlling you, then do the same thing another half-dozen times or so.

When that's done, you're really getting close to setting yourself completely free, because you're teaching your brain that what has happened in the past actually has no bearing on what happens in the future... Unless you actually want it to.

Can't versus won't...

One of the most common reactions to contemplating doing something like the above, something that is different from what others would normally expect of you is: *"I can't do that!"* It's actually a fake response and one which needs to be changed as soon as possible because the problem with 'can't' in this context is that it's a no-choice word – it restricts you to doing only what you've always done. And that old saying: 'if you always do what you've always done, you'll always get what you always got," is absolutely correct.

So change things around and say *"I won't do that!"* instead and straight away you have choice. You are in control of your life, deciding that you won't take a particular course of action even though you could if you wished. It's better still if you say: *"I won't do that, because..."* and fill in the dots with the reason. That gives you even more autonomy, since you can state the case for your choice and it's nobody's business but yours. It's empowering, the more so if you allow yourself to recognise the Great Truth that you actually can do whatever you like (ignoring things like jumping over a ten-foot high wall and crushing rocks with your bare hands.) The only hindrance is whatever the price might be – because there always *is* a price. But there's often a reward as well.

Let's test the idea a few times – and if your particular 'won't' doesn't appear here, you'll still get the idea and be able to test it for yourself.

- *"I won't wear a red jacket because I'd feel silly."* Okay... So the price is feeling silly but you could still do it if you wanted to. You could pursue this further by investigating exactly why you'd 'feel silly' to see if that was valid or it was just a belief that you've never tested.
- *"I won't stand up to my boss because I might lose my job."* So, the price of this one is that you need to seek a new job. The reward is that you'd be starting on a fresh footing. A relationship might have the same issue.
- *"I won't do karaoke because people will laugh at my voice."* No problem – you can do karaoke and let them laugh – that's the price. Laughing with them will endear you to them and that's the reward.
- *"I won't talk to my partner about sex because it's embarrassing."* Well, maybe it is and that's the price – but you can still do it. The reward is most likely better sex.

The interesting thing is that once you re-qualify a 'can't' to a 'won't' and actually start doing the thing anyway, it actually is nowhere near as daunting as you might have first thought. The reward will be even more powerful though, as a result of the sense of achievement. Just for fun, think through one of your own particular 'won'ts' and ask yourself if the 'won't' is genuinely valid and what would happen if you did it anyway. And what would happen then? And what would the reward be?

Then re-evaluate it to see if the 'won't' is as strong as it was to start with – it's odds-on that it won't be!

At this point, all the basic preparation has been made for you to finally break free from the prison that has held you but there's something very important that you have to do first: accept **once and for all** that you will give up the whole idea of using depression to get you 'off the hook', get you out of doing things, or to try to get attention... which doesn't make you feel any better anyway.

The quote from the beginning of this chapter is important enough to say again: *If you want to get attention, do it the right way – be impressive!*

Chapter Twelve

The past is a different country...

'The past is a different county... they do things differently there' was never so true as when you're moving away from the world of depression into a more uplifted life. They certainly do things differently *there.*

In some ways it's as if you're moving to a whole different part of the world where the culture, the language, and the people are unfamiliar; you need to learn new customs, a new language and a new way of being. The only difference is that the change will be more gradual, so that you have time to make the transition at your own pace. This might all sound a bit silly but it's a certainty that as people you know begin to notice you're different, they'll behave differently towards you. In fact, they will gradually begin to behave towards you as they do to everybody else who they consider to be 'normal'. Here are some of the things you might notice:

- They stop asking how you are in *that* voice
- They stop making allowances for you, expecting the same from you as they do from others
- If you heave a great sigh, they might say: *"What's up?"* instead of: *"Oh dear..."* or: *"Never mind..."*
- They start including you in their plans
- They start to ask your opinion on all sorts of things
- They start to become interested in what you have to say
- They start to seek out your company instead of trying to avoid it!

This is something that has been mentioned earlier in the book, but it's worth repeating here: *Many people suffering from depression often feel left out of things; they turn on the 'depression tap' a bit more, seeking to get attention, but all that happens is that people become ever more keen not to get involved.*

Now, this might seem rather cruel to you but there's a very good and totally natural reason for it, in that people run out of ideas. They feel they can't keep saying the same thing all the time and feel as if they should somehow be more inventive or be the same as they wrongly imagine everybody else is. This leads to them feeling inadequate (a feeling that you might even know quite well) and so they seek to avoid the source of discomfort. You. Either that or they don't really listen to what you're saying and rattle on about their own stuff instead.

The longer you've been depressed, the longer people have experienced your depression, the more of an uphill struggle it can be to leave the past back where it belongs and move into the shiny new future you're looking for. But don't get depressed about that! It's totally normal for people to either not notice the changes in you or to suspect that 'it won't last' and so for a while, they want to keep their distance. You can get past almost all of it in one fell swoop by the simple expedient of *telling* them that you've read a book, done some exercises, and now it's time for you to join the real world again. Or, if you like, you can say 'join the real world **at last**' instead of 'again' if it's been going on for so long nobody remembers you ever being any different.

Anyway, we've still got a bit of work to do to cement what you've already done into place, to strengthen it so that others cannot fail to notice it and start to think of you as an equal.

Development check: *How do you feel about people thinking of you as an equal? If the answer is not a resounding 'Good!' work out what you're still trying to use the depression for and deal with it. Before reading any further, in fact, because it's essential that you've managed to let go of those hidden agendas if you're to get the best out of all the work you're doing.*

Some more questions...

Still here? Good. Right, now there are some more questions for you to answer, though this time you don't need to write the answers down – but you do need to make sure you answer every one of them, even if it gets a little uncomfortable. Uncomfortable is just as much a part of not being depressed as it is of being depressed, in fact. The questions are in groups of related ideas:

Group one: Who's the most lovable person you know? What made you decide that? Do other people always find them lovable? How did you find that out? Does anybody not like them at all? How do you know that? (Call this one 'Person A'.)

Group two: Who's the *least* lovable person you know? What is it about them that makes you realise that? Would everybody else agree with you? Are you sure about that? Do some people love them? If 'Yes' what do you think about that? If 'No', how do you know that? (Call this one 'Person B')

Group three: Which one of the two are you most like? What made you realise that? Do you have elements of *both* 'Person A' and 'Person B' in your character? What do you think people *would* like about "Person B'? How much like that are you? What do you think would people *not* like about 'Person A?' How much like that are you?

Make sure you've answered all those questions as completely as you can before trying to answer this last one: **What do you think people think of you?**

If you completed the task properly, there's only one valid answer to that last question, and that is: *"I don't know."* And that's the point. You cannot possibly know what people think of you and this exercise should have helped you to realise that – and it is a Very Important Fact! The truth of it is that you cannot answer for 'people' though you might get it right now and again if you were thinking about what certain individuals thought of you. Only now and again though. Most of the time you would be astonished what they really thought, because the truth is that none of us see others as they really are – we see them as *we think they are* and that will only be a reflection of what we think of ourselves. Not only that, it's a fair bet that you have something of 'Person A' about you and also elements of 'Person B'. So that muddies the waters even more! In the normal way, we tend to not like people who we believe think they are better than us, instead liking people who we believe think of us as equals. We don't think too much about the rest. That's in the normal way. Sometimes, though, ego takes a different angle and then we still don't like those who we believe think they are better than us, but like those who we think look up to us in some way, and not think much about the others...

But however you look at it, for every hundred people you meet, it's a pretty safe bet that thirty will like you, thirty won't like you, and the other forty won't care much one way or the other! In fact, it might be even less in the like/don't like categories, because that's the way life is. We tend to notice the things we really don't like and the things we really *do* like in people and then form our assessment of them on that basis only. We are simply not aware of the rest of their particular way of being, so much so that people can sometimes catch us by surprise by behaving 'out of character'. The truth, though, is they are not behaving out of character at all – they are just exhibiting a side of themselves we hadn't noticed before. But the oddest thing is, it doesn't usually change our opinion of them – we still either like or dislike them because that's the way we work. Almost unbelievably, we often decide whether we like or dislike a person purely on the basis of the first few things we first notice about them, and once our mind's made up we don't change it very easily. In fact, we will quite often vigorously defend our choice to those who disagree with us.

Hopefully the last few paragraphs have helped you to realise that you don't actually have to change the way you are – only how you feel... And you've already done a lot towards that particular task and are probably already feeling the benefits of your labours. So now we're going to move on to a different subject altogether, one that might or might not be relevant to you but without which this book would not be complete.

Grief

Grief is a very strange situation indeed and intensely personal, so that what affects one person severely just doesn't touch another. We're not necessarily talking about grief over a lost relative or companion, but about *any* loss at all. It's surprising how many times the pain of grief fades into the background but is never really resolved, sitting in the subconscious and stealing positive energy from the psyche. One of the most common effects of this is – and you've probably already guessed it – Depression. Hence its inclusion here, though since this is not a book about grief, there is only really enough here for you to gain an understanding of the importance of letting go of what you need to. Often, just the understanding is enough to complete the task but when it's not, there are a good few professional therapists who will be able to help you once you recognise that you need that help.

Grief is simply the response we get when someone or some*thing* we love is taken from us when we were not ready for it to happen. It doesn't matter if the loss was expected or not – 'not being ready' has got little or nothing to do with the circumstances in which you experience the loss, but everything to do with a highly complex emotional response. The 'normal' pattern it follows is: *Denial, Anger, Depression, Acceptance* – but getting to that final stage of Acceptance, where pain stops, is sometimes difficult. Even more complicated is the fact that it doesn't follow a logical pattern at all. *Denial* is almost always the first reaction, and might be just the word: *"No!"* to begin with. Then there will often be *Anger* which might be directed at carers (doctors, nurses, surgeons and so on), self, another person, or even the deceased. That can so easily be followed by the sudden onset of more Denial – *"I keep on thinking they'll turn up as if nothing had happened at any minute!"* or: *"I thought I saw them in the back garden, large as life."*

So those first three stages can flip flop backwards and forwards for a long time, protecting the psyche from the final stage of *Acceptance*. It might seem an odd thing that the mind seeks to avoid the comfort and cessation of pain that comes with Acceptance – until you recognise that the other three stages all carry a connection to the deceased. There may be a subconscious hope that it wasn't real, just a dream... and acceptance is the recognition of finality.

The loss might be for a person, a pet (much more common than some people think) or even for one's own lost childhood. It's not necessarily even about physical death, but can be over the breakup of a relationship, the pain of which can sometimes be worse than if there had been a physical death. It can even be over the loss of a home or a work relationship that has been especially close or lengthy.

Usually, grief takes about eighteen months to two years for the mind to deal with, at the end of which time you should have found, or be close to, a sense of acceptance that that part of your life is no more. But if you still feel 'raw' after two years or longer have passed, or a sense that something just wasn't right, or if the memory seems to trigger or worsen the depression, then it's likely that you are suffering *unresolved* grief. Understanding what you are reading here might help you to complete the task. If there has been a physical death, it's usually easier to accept the finality of it; anything you didn't say cannot now be heard; anything you didn't do cannot now be done; anything you did do cannot now be undone. **It's over and it's time to move on, accept that things were the way they were because of what was relevant at the time, and get on with the process of living.**

On the other hand, if there was no physical death then you still have the same task of acceptance. This time though, you need to carry the recognition that even if you went back to wherever you wish you were, all it would mean is that you would have to go through the whole thing again. If you broke up with somebody once, there was a reason for it at the time and no matter how much you regret it, the breakup will have caused damage that cannot be completely repaired – there's always a 'shadow' of the problem lurking in the background, because the brain never forgets such an event.

As stated before, this is not a book about grief or the resolution of it, more a kind of clarification to help you understand how it can affect, even cause, many forms of depression. If you now believe you are suffering from the aftermath of grief, seek out the services of a grief counsellor – an Internet search will reveal many in your area, almost certainly.

The power of meditation

It has long been established that meditation reduces stress and depression – over time it even changes the structure of the physical brain and the way it works. The problem for most people, though, is they're not actually sure what meditation is, how to do it, or what to do while they *are* doing it. Well, you're going to learn a very special form of meditation now, using specific energy points in the body that many people know as Chakra points, sometimes called Chakra *knots*. They are part of Hindu and yogic tradition and culture, and are located where there is a branching of nerves or blood vessels in the physical body, though Chakras are part of what is called the 'subtle body' which is *non*-physical. Although the word is Sanskrit in origin (it means 'wheel' or 'turning'), in the yogic context it translates to 'vortex' or 'whirlpool' which indicates why we use it for meditation: *to calm the whirlpool.*

Here, though, we're not going in for anything at all mystical, instead just using those Chakras as points of focus to get you into a good meditative state. The end result will feel rather similar to, but far deeper than, what you've already been doing in the 'breathing thing' to find the quiet moment of now. As mentioned before, that itself is a mild form of what is known as 'mindfulness' meditation – but this is going to be an improvement on that no end.

So what you are going to learn here is in effect a kind of 'deluxe' version of what you've already done a good few times as you've read this book. Or should have done, anyway, if you've been behaving yourself. You don't need to write anything down for this and though it will be done with your eyes closed it is simplicity itself to remember, since we use a concept with which you are probably already very familiar – the colours of the rainbow.

You might already know the mnemonic 'device' for remembering the order of those colours: **Richard Of York Gave Battle In Vain** – Red, Orange, Yellow, Green, Blue, Indigo, Violet. We're going to use only the first six of those, and in reverse order: Indigo, Blue, Green, Yellow, Orange, Red. Those colours have been used in connection with meditation and the Chakra points for thousands of years. We're going to focus on the first six of the seven that are considered to be the most important – we don't use the 'Crown' point in the centre of the scalp (usually considered to be of the purest white), since it is not relevant to the simple meditation exercise given here. The six are, with their colours:

- The middle of the forehead (the 'third eye') and indigo
- The throat and blue
- The middle of the chest and green (though some 'see' pink here)
- The solar plexus and yellow

- The belly (more correctly the sacral area of the spine) and orange
- The base of the spine and red

It's worth spending a few minutes memorising those pairs – the order is easy because it's simply top downwards. Third eye – indigo; throat – blue; chest – green; solar plexus – yellow; belly – orange; base of the spine – red.

Now for a little practice. With your eyes closed, think of those energy points and their associated colours slowly, one at a time for just a few seconds each. If you forget, that's not a problem, just open your eyes to remind yourself of the sequence and start again. It is important, though, that you can go confidently from the first to the sixth without forgetting the colour or losing your place, so keep practising until it becomes so easy it's almost boring! Choose the tones of colour that you like – if you like an electric blue for the throat, for instance, use that; if you're happier with the colour of a pale winter sky then that's fine too. If you like pink instead of green for the chest point, use that. In other words, make sure you are completely comfortable with each colour before continuing the exercise.

The exercise

Right, now you're ready to do the exercise itself and though you will need to remember it before trying it, you've already completed the most difficult part of it – remembering the sequence of colours and energy points. If the idea of the spiritual values mentioned, as associated with some of the energy points, doesn't really resonate with you, don't worry – just concentrate on the colours and your breathing as shown. It will work every bit as well for you as it needs to. So:

1. Think of the third eye, be aware of your breathing, and imagine or think of the colour indigo. Wait for a little

while to see if you can find it but if it doesn't happen, don't worry. It probably will next time but if you haven't found it after a couple of minutes or so, move on to the next step. If you do find it, stay there until you feel you want to move on. Some people say that imagining breathing through this point helps you receive love from the Universe.

2.   Move your thoughts down to your throat now, searching for the colour blue, again waiting for a little while to find it but not being concerned if you don't. You might find only one or two of the colours at first but later you will probably eventually find them all. If you do find it, as with the previous one, imagine that you can breathe through that point. Many mystics believe that if you can vividly imagine breathing through each energy point, you are opening them and your mind to the best of psychological, spiritual and bodily health. Move on to the next step when you're ready.

3.   The chest now, waiting for the colour green (or pink if that just happens automatically, or if you prefer it) and again, imagining you can breathe through this point. This one is important because it's associated with the heart and breathing through here opens your psyche to give and receive feelings of romantic love, according to those who agree with the ancient teachings.

4.   When you're ready, move your thoughts down to the solar plexus now, the area just beneath the sternum and above the navel. Search for, or think about, the colour yellow here. Again, focus on your breathing while you're here and if you can find the colour, imagine you can breathe easily through this energy point. By now, you'll be just starting to feel a slight change of state, rather like when you close your eyes and listen to the television instead of watch it, or when you are awake but

comfortably relaxed behind your closed eyelids.

5. The next stage is the sacral chakra and it's associated with the colour orange. For some reason, many people find it easier to vividly imagine orange than any of the other colours when they first try this particular meditative technique; if you do find it, imagine breathing through it but if you don't just concentrate on your breathing while you think about what it might be like if you *could* 'see' the orange colour.

6. The final point now, the base of the spine, associated with the colour red. The ancients referred to this point as 'Kundalini' – the sleeping, dormant force of the human psyche. Imagining the colour red here whilst concentrating on your breathing can create an enormous sense of well-being and personal autonomy. Stay here for a while, even if you cannot find the colour, noticing the way your breath feels as it enters and leaves your body.

7. Stay quietly where you are, being aware only of your breathing and whatever colours, if any, you can see or imagine. You'll find a quiet stillness that is more profound than anything you acquired doing just the 'breathing thing' on its own. At first, you might find it difficult to stay in this place for very long but it will get easier the more you practise. When you have managed to achieve the full meditative state, there's no need to attempt to do anything with it – that's the secret of getting the best out of it. Just be with yourself, aware of yourself and your breathing... And eventually you will cease to be even aware of your breathing, instead just being at one with yourself and a calm mind.

If images come to mind during this time, whether they are pleasant, not so pleasant or completely benign, give them no importance, instead just letting them drift through your mind and depart again, as if they were nothing more than clouds floating through your senses. This becomes steadily easier each time you practise this technique – and it is a good idea to set aside a certain time each day for it. It can be as short as fifteen minutes or so, or as long as an hour; when you start, know in your mind the time you want to leave the state and your mind will rouse you at that point.

Some general advice for meditation: a quiet place is best but not essential; spend as long on each point as you feel you want to; if your mind starts to drift, bring it back to the task as soon as you notice it (this often happens with beginners to meditation); accept that what you find or feel at any one session is exactly right – it is what it is and there's absolutely nothing to be gained from wanting it to be something else.

And now it's time to move on to the final stage of setting you free for life!

Embracing Change

Getting ready to be in charge of your life

And here we are at the last stage of the 'beating the hell out of depression' part of the book because the next part is all about continuing to improve for the rest of your life. We still have a little bit of work to do, though, to finalise some of the processes that have been started in the background – and don't worry about it if you're not too sure that they *have* started, because that's how many people feel. But think back to how you were when you started reading this book and compare it with now... And as long as you completed all the exercises, there will be a difference. It might well feel so 'normal', though, that it seems to be unremarkable. That happens often, too!

Those background changes might actually be among the most important because they will have started you on the path of *wanting* to get away from the old self and living a full life. That doesn't mean it's going to be happy, happy, happy because life really *isn't* like that. 'Living a full life' means living inside of yourself *and with* what you're doing, instead of just watching others apparently getting on with things. It means recognising and enjoying the good bits and accepting and weathering the not-so-good bits... because they're just as important a part of life as anything else.

Chapter Thirteen

So you think you have a choice...

What you are about to read might surprise you – and puzzle you, too, because it appears to contradict so much of what you have already read in this book. The advice you've been receiving so far is that you actually have a choice about the way you conduct your life and that's true... but only to an extent.

The surprising truth is that although you might *think* you have free will and can make your own decisions whenever you want to, you actually haven't. Well, not in the way you might think, anyway. Now before you go getting all despairing, do read on for a few pages and you'll discover just how exciting this news actually is!

To cut straight to the amazing truth – any course of action is decided by your physical brain more than one-third of a second before you are consciously aware of what you are going to do. We've touched on this before but now it's time for the full description. To clarify (because you might not believe what you're reading otherwise), whatever you decide to do, think or say has been decided by your physical brain before you know what it is you're going to do, think or say. Of course, you might now be thinking: *"Well, that's all very interesting, but I can just change my mind whenever I want to."* Well, of course you can. But that decision was also made before you were aware of it...

Later in this chapter, you'll discover the scientific proof of all this and also find out how to use this rather odd situation to complete the changework that you been involved in since the start of the book. First, though, it's important to recognise that there's nothing odd or 'spooky' about any of it. It's not about some spiritual belief that everything is preordained or that our lives just run in a continuous loop, or that the whole of existence is just an illusion. It's actually much simpler than that. It's all about the speed with which our brains work, in comparison with how slow our thoughts are by comparison.

It's a fact that the brain continually monitors everything around us and within us (and it encounters millions of things every second) and assesses it to see if any action is indicated. If it finds something familiar, it will try to take the same action as it did the previous time, as long as it led to survival (and it did, because you're still here!) But there's a problem. The brain is completely impartial and unbiased, and doesn't have any 'value judgment' at the beginning – that comes much later, when we become consciously aware of what's going on. It doesn't know or care if what it starts to do is what you actually want or not... If it's done that thing before, it will attempt to do it again. Now, it's obviously a little bit more complicated than that but this isn't a book about brain science!

Another startling fact is that before it enters conscious awareness, the information the brain has been working with travels around 50 metres of neural pathways before we are aware of it, all the time being tested for a recognised response pattern. And guess what... If nothing is found, nothing is activated and as a result, we just don't know what to do – it means it's something we've never experienced before! It causes discomfort because unknown situations can be potentially unsafe. Here are a few things, though, that illustrate the brain working faster than your conscious thoughts and finding a response pattern:

- If a ball was lobbed towards you, you would instinctively try to catch it.
- If a ball was thrown hard *at* you, you would instinctively try to dodge it.
- If an insect flies at your face, you close your eyes without thinking.
- Emergency braking when driving.

- Putting your arms out for balance if you start to fall.
- Trying to catch something you've dropped before it hits the floor.

And how about that thing at amusement parks where people stand behind a glass screen at the water chute, yet *still* duck when water sprays towards them as the car goes through, even though they know there's glass there! You can probably think of more examples but you get the idea. It's highly likely that what used to be considered the 'subconscious' is actually the physical brain...

*So how does all this affect you? Well, if the brain assesses that some input or another should be met with the depression response, that's what you'll get. You won't necessarily know **why** though, or what triggered it. It could even be that once, a long time ago, it got you attention or allowed you to escape some sort of task. It doesn't matter that it's no longer relevant or that you don't want it – the brain doesn't make that sort of assessment.*

Fortunately, it's possible to make changes to what the brain puts into action and we've already been working at that. Soon, we're going to have a look at the most powerful method *ever* of making those changes, now that you've already started to truly want to be free and even made efforts towards it. First though, the science behind these rather outrageous claims... But if you aren't interested in the technical stuff, that's okay – just skip the next section and go straight to the **Brainwork** heading.

Benjamin Libet's experiments

In 1983, a scientist by the name of Benjamin Libet was carrying out tests to see how long it took motor nerves (the ones that make your muscles work) to respond after the decision to move was made. His test subjects were hooked up to an EEG machine, which measures brain activity, and placed in front of a dial with a dot moving around the outer edge. They were asked to note the position of the dot on the numbered dial at the precise moment they decided to move a finger. To his surprise, he observed that the brain was preparing to 'fire' the nerve paths (creating a 'readiness potential') over half a second before the subjects reported the number; and actually 'fired' the nerves (the 'action potential') more than a third of a second before the test subjects were consciously aware of the decision having been made. Put simply, if it was reported that the decision was made when the dot hit the '9', say, the brain had started the process before the dot had even reached the '8'! He repeated the experiments, as so many have done since, and achieved the same results.

The test subjects *felt* as if they were making the choice consciously, since the 'brainwork' is invisible to us; but the fact remains that over and again, the tests showed that the relevant neural paths began to activate more than half-a-second before the individual was aware of it.

Brainwork

So we're going to use this interesting phenomenon constructively to see if we can deal with the very roots of the depression – and as long as you are able to remember one time which triggered or worsened the feeling, you are set to go. Almost, anyway, because there's one other important bit of information we need. You might remember reading, in Chapter Four, about the 'gems' that your subconscious can come up with, given the right trigger. It was in relation to the way the word 'but' is used and here are the two important phrases that illustrate the importance of that 'but' word.

- *"I'd like to do more with my life but this depression makes it difficult."*
- *"This depression makes it difficult but I'm going to do more with my life."*

The second phrase, you will remember, prompts the subconscious/brain to start seeking a solution and you were advised that you should write down every idea that occurred to you, no matter how unhelpful they were. If you did that, you will indeed have encountered some 'gems' which we'll be using shortly in an exercise that will get that speedy brain of yours focussed onto thoughts and feelings that are helpful, instead of destructive. It's actually one of the most powerful ways of working and the subject of a new therapy model launched in 2013 by the author of this book, called **BrainWorking Recursive Therapy®** (BWRT® for short.) It's impossible to make use of the full process here but we can certainly create a 'lite' version which, after the work you've now completed, will give a kickstart to the new you! So let's get started – well, as long as you did that exercise mentioned earlier, about writing down every idea that came to mind. If you did, you can skip the next section and go straight to the **Doing it** heading. Otherwise, there's a bit of work still to do.

I didn't do it

Okay, the first thing to recognise is that you're not the only one who has to read this section before they can continue. You'll be able to resolve the problem shortly but first, here's something you must take to heart if you are to get to where you seem to want to go. You apparently want to get better, or you wouldn't be reading this book... But you also apparently don't really want to have to do too much yourself to get there! Depression is a tricky place to get away from and many people just want others to somehow make them better. This is totally understandable in many ways; depression saps energy, creates feelings of 'I don't think I can be bothered', and often encourages a feeling that no matter what you do, nothing will work because you're just no good at stuff. You might remember reading about just this sort of thing near the beginning of the book.

The problem is there are only three things you can do with depression:

- Take medication (which often doesn't work or has side effects)
- Put up with it for the rest of your life
- Do something positive about fixing it

There isn't a fourth option. If you wait for somebody to come up with something else that works without you having to do anything, you're in for a very long wait, unfortunately... Many people will have been reading this book and deciding that they'll do something with the ideas and exercises 'one day.' But the truth is that they'll get to the end of it, declare that it didn't work and either throw it away or plonk it in a drawer somewhere where it will soon be forgotten about altogether.

So you have an important choice to make now. A Very Important Choice. If the writing things down bit of the 'but reversal' exercise was the only thing you didn't do, that's not too bad because you'll be able to sort that out very shortly. If, though, you've done hardly any (or none) of the exercises then the only thing you can do if you want the programme to work for you – and it *does* work – is to go back to the start and do the exercises in the order they are presented. You don't need to read the whole thing again, of course, just enough to complete the exercises successfully. Or you can decide not to bother... It's your choice. But if you take the 'not to bother' option, do at least take the trouble to read Chapter Three again before finalising that decision – it might just give you the extra little bit of help you need to get onto the right track to good emotional health.

If it was only the one exercise you didn't do, you can sort that out now; it might not be *quite* as good as if you had done the original exercise but it can still be astonishingly effective. Think for a moment about that one time when something triggered the depression or made it worse – and the worse one you can find, the better. It will only be in your mind for a moment or two and we're going to actually *use* that memory to help you so don't worry that it might somehow undo everything you've worked on. Quite the reverse will happen, in fact, because you will soon be stripping that memory of every bit of apparent power it has. Or rather, *used* to have...

Do the 'breathing thing' to find the quiet moment of now, then let your mind drift to how you would have preferred to react to whatever the trigger event was. Perhaps you would have liked it to have been just like 'water off a duck's back'. Maybe you would prefer to have recognised that whatever it was, was of no great consequence in terms of a lifetime. You can even decide that you would just dismiss the whole thing as not really being relevant to you, when you had a good look at it. You can choose any reaction you like but it must be something that is designed to help *you*, rather than punish somebody else, and must also be realistic. If what you choose couldn't possibly have happened, then your brain will know that and what you are about to do just won't work. For instance, shrugging off an insult and being unaffected by it would be good; finding a sparkling bit of repartee that left you feeling triumphant would certainly be realistic; but kicking the person in the shins and running off laughing just about breaks all the rules! Whatever you end up with is your 'gem' for later.

Okay, do the breathing thing now and find your preferred response. Sit with it for a while and see if it changes and if it remains constant for a couple of minutes or so, you're now ready to continue with the 'therapy', though you'll start on the second paragraph of the next section.

Doing it

So, take the best of those 'gems' that your subconscious came up with... It was actually the brain that gave it to you of course, so it's already primed to respond favourably.

Close your eyes now and make a mental note of where you feel it in your body and also notice in how much of your body you can feel it. It might be just in a small place or it could seem as if it's all over – and it could even feel as if it surrounds you like an aura of some sort. Notice if it seems to be associated with a colour, sound or scent. Whatever comes naturally to you is exactly the right thing for you, even if that is just the 'gem' and nothing else at all. There's nothing to be gained from forcing anything else into the work, since it will not be part of what your brain naturally does. Remember, your brain is ahead of your thoughts all the time! Make sure you have this 'gem' firmly in your mind before you continue.

So now we move onto the next stage. You'll need to remember the whole of the section in italics and fortunately, there's not too much of it – it is important to get it right though, so read it through a few times before attempting the actual exercise itself.

*Remember that one time, the worst one you can recall, of when something either triggered or worsened the depression... Make it vivid enough that it starts to feel uncomfortable... now zoom in to the worst part of that worst memory, to just one pinpoint in time, and **freeze** that moment in time so that it's as if it's nothing more than a sterile image, perhaps like a waxwork... And when you freeze it like that **every scrap** of feeling that was mixed up with that memory just stops... Because emotional responses can't exist when time stops... Now bring in the feeling that's connected to that 'gem', and then let whatever you recalled continue from the freeze moment onwards, but with the new feelings, until it's complete... It doesn't need to be more than a few seconds and you're then at the moment of 'now' with the new feeling... Let the 'gem' feelings be in or around your body with any colours, sounds or scents that you found... Stay with that for just a few seconds, then you can shoot the whole feeling forwards to sometime in the future... a week, perhaps... or a day or a year... the choice is yours, but vividly imagine telling someone just* *exactly how **well** you feel... Then loop that back to the 'freeze' memory and go through the whole thing again, six or seven times, speeding up the whole time and not thinking too much about it, finishing on the moment of 'now' and just resting, doing nothing for a couple of minutes... When you decide to open your eyes again, test that original recall that felt so bad... It should have hardly any of the feeling left now and so the job's done...*

And that's it. To help you remember it, here's a 'nutshell' version of it:

1.   Find the worst memory
2.   Freeze the worst part
3.   Notice how it stops everything
4.   Get the feelings of your 'gem'
5.   Carry them to the moment of 'now'
6.   Shoot the feeling forwards to the future

Loop back to (3) and repeat six times, finishing at (4) when you rest for a couple of minutes.

Do make certain you have it clearly in your mind before you actually start to do the exercise; this one needs you to be so conversant with it you can run through it without having to think – it relies on *speed* for those loops.

As already mentioned, this is just a 'lite' version of the new BrainWorking Recursive Therapy® but if you prepare properly, and are sure to freeze that moment in time, you can get an excellent result. There's nothing that can go catastrophically wrong but there are a couple of places where you *might* find a problem, so the following is a kind of 'trouble shooting' guide:

- **Can't freeze the memory:** This is almost always because you're not working in exactly the right part of the recall, *or* it's not really the worst recall. Drift through the memory again and find the bit that feels worst and freeze it, which will stop any uncomfortable feelings in their tracks.

- **The memory keeps on changing:** This happens sometimes and all it means is that there are several 'triggers' of roughly equal strength. In that case, just decide which one you want to work on. You can work through others later if you want to because there's no limit on how many times you can do this.

- **I'm not sure about the 'moment of now':** That's just the moment where you are. As you're reading this, you're in a moment of now. After you've created the freeze and brought in your 'gem', you can just let whatever you recalled play through in your mind but with the new feelings. It might look like a film in your mind, or you might imagine being there but as long as you are keeping the new feelings connected to it, it doesn't matter which.

- **I can't shoot the feeling forward:** Just imagine telling somebody later on – somebody you know, perhaps – how well you're feeling after doing some self-help stuff a little while ago. Essentially, what you're doing here is remembering something that hasn't happened yet... But your brain won't know that! Whatever you imagine, as long as it's vivid enough, your brain will assume it as a reality. And if you're remembering getting well, the brain will adopt the new feelings of wellness and make them real.

- **There's still a lot of negativity attached to the trigger:** Do the whole process again, another six times. The feeling will diminish each time – it cannot *not* – and there's no limit on the number of loops.

- **I've got a lot of miserable memories:** Do the same process with each of them! You can use the same 'gem' feeling or choose a different one each time.

- **It didn't seem to do much:** Speed is very important. The loops have to be completed as fast as possible without any assessment – analysing what's happening is inclined to inhibit the process. Some people find it difficult to avoid this but practice makes it easier. If you find it impossible to avoid, you could benefit from working with a professional **BWRT® Practitioner** – go to: http://www.bwrt.org to find one.

In the next chapter, you are going to see how you can really start to bring together the work you've been doing up until now – there are more questions for you to answer, too, but this time every single one of them is empowering!

Chapter Fourteen

The wisdom of the ancients

The Maya civilisation (c. 2000 BC—AD 900) was astonishing in many ways. They had the first fully developed written language in South America and astounding knowledge of mathematics and astronomy, as well as being highly developed in matters of art and architecture. Their influences can be found as far away as central Mexico, some thousand kilometres away from the central Maya area.

They were a fascinating people and many books have been written about them but what we are going to concentrate on here, just for a little while, is a very specific and powerful concept. They held that the entire human race was in effect a huge and perfectly tuned machine; that every part of it was vital in some way, and if any part was destroyed, it would change the way the machine functioned. It makes sense, when you think of it, since people are being born and people are dying all the time; the population is steadily increasing and The Machine is steadily evolving and becoming ever more complex as more parts are added... But still each part is vital for The Machine to continue to function in the way it has been doing.

It's a nice concept – it doesn't only work for the whole of humanity, but also on a much smaller scale. You can apply it to your own immediate world of family and friends, tormentors and criticisers, helpers and hinderers and everybody else you can think of. It might seem to you that if you were to remove a tormentor, your life would improve... And yet, what if that tormentor is one of the reasons that's motivating you to find a way out of depression? Not only that, but just for a moment, think about that exercise where it was established that everybody is liked by some people and disliked by others. Your tormentor has a machine, too, which you are a distinct part of, and they also are part of other people's machines...so it's complicated! You can probably see that if you tried to remove or change any part of that Machine, it would work differently in some way, though it's just about impossible to predict what sort of difference it would be. It certainly would not leave you in control of your life! So now perhaps you can see why the *only* reliable change you can make is to you – you are in control of that and so any changes that it makes to your machine will work perfectly for you. Now, that means that it is inevitable that you will be instrumental in changing the lives of others in some small way as you change. Maybe in a big way, if they're emotionally close to you. So what you're actually doing here is changing your world, which is exciting!

And now we're going to narrow your personal Machine down even further, to the Machine that is your brain. More precisely, your thoughts, the product of that Machine. The same 'Machine rules' apply though – change or remove any one part and the whole thing works differently... So we need to make sure the changes you make produce the best result. The good news is that you've been doing precisely that (or should have!) since the beginning of this book! It started in Chapter One when you stopped referring to 'My' depression and instead used 'The' depression. (You *did* do that didn't you?) And it culminated in the exercise in the last chapter when you learnt how to use the self-help version of BrainWorking Recursive Therapy®

So, most of the work is done now. Don't worry if you're not yet feeling as if anything special has happened (though it's probable that you're feeling quite a lot better than you were when you started the book.) The work has been done but we've still yet to focus it and that's the task you're about to begin...

The plan

Don't worry – in spite of the heading of this section you haven't got to do yet more exercises and make more plans. All you have to do, in fact, is to answer a whole lot of questions in your mind because the plan is going to be in your imagination only. You can write your answers down if you prefer and it's likely that it will make the task of focussing work in the most effective way possible. It's not essential though, especially if you have a powerful imagination. So, on to the starting point for this whole section:

Planning for success

The first question: *If you knew beyond doubt that success was inevitable, what would you do?*

Let your mind run as wild as you like here. You're not required to actually put the plan into action, as you will see, so you can be quite extravagant in your choice... But now here's a reminder of something you've already read in Chapter Ten but which is Very Important: whatever you choose as success must be **plausible** (that is, it is definitely something that is doable); it must be **possible** (i.e. it must be within your genuine capabilities); and it must be **fair** (that is, it is designed purely to improve your life and not to hinder that of anybody else.) Plausible, possible and fair are the criteria you should use for any plan that you ever create, as a matter of fact, because it genuinely makes success more likely, thanks to the way the brain works. The plan can be for material gain, for relationships, for emotional stability or anything else you choose but it must be something you could put into action yourself. So bearing these points in mind, vividly create your plan for the future before continuing.

The second question: *What will that feel like when you have achieved it?* You'll notice that this question is phrased as if you will actually be putting the plan into action and this is to keep it as realistic as possible. As you consider your answer, let yourself imagine that you have achieved your objective and you are now thoroughly enjoying the results of all your hard work. What will it feel like? Again, keep it plausible, possible and focussed determinedly on *you*. As before, complete the task before moving on to the next stage – do that with every question here, in fact.

The third question: *Who will do their best to help you? How will they do that?*

You can choose 'nobody', a best friend, a family member, or simply recognise that you need to get a professional to help you. A therapist or life-coach, perhaps. Maybe a business advisor or financial consultant. The bank, maybe. Remember, this is all to stretch your imagination and focus your thinking processes so, once again, in your mind you can employ the best person you can, if you need to. Or you could just use your powers of persuasion and whatever encouragement is needed, if any, to get the best person you know for the task 'on side'. Whoever you choose, even if you are going it alone, decide how they (or you) will do whatever is necessary to ensure success as far as is possible. If they need to use a skill that you know nothing about, then recognise that situation as a vulnerability and work out what you would do to ensure that you are as safe as possible.

The fourth question: *Who will try to stop you? Why and how will they do that?*

It's likely that you knew the answer to this triple question as soon as you read it, or at least two-thirds of it – many people do. But if that's not the case, don't run away with the idea that everybody will be rooting for you because they won't! Your success will change other people's Machines and one or some of them will make efforts to resist that change if it's not beneficial to them. If you were going to open a shoe shop, for instance, anybody you know (or even somebody you don't know for that matter) who owns a shoe shop will want to stop you taking their trade. If you are doing a real number on yourself to become a sparkling member of your family, the one who is already the sparkling member might well suffer jealousy and do their best to hinder your transformational efforts. It might sound cynical, perhaps, but it *is* how the world works much of the time. So the 'who', 'why' and 'how' are the important parts of this question.

The fifth question: *Will you let them? How will you stop them if not?*

It's *really* to be hoped that your answer to the first part of this double question is a resounding *"No!"* If you find yourself thinking that you wouldn't be able to stop them, have another think! Anything is possible in your mind – remember to keep it realistic and legal but don't shy away from using the forces of the law if necessary. Or if you believe a family rift would happen as a result, for example, then recognise that rift as being as much the other's doing as yours. You have as many rights as any other individual to make positive changes in your life; others have the right to object to those changes if they are directly affected by them, or even if they just don't like them. This is the way the world works. It might be an example of how your life used to work and if you don't want the confrontation, you can buckle and return to that original 'normality', or you can stand your ground and shoulder the consequences – it's your choice. That is also how the world works. Remember, this is an exploration of the Machine that is your mind – give it a thorough test!

The sixth question: *What would happen then? How would you deal with that?*

It's important to consider the fact that although most dissent 'blows over', especially when it's over minor things, this is not always the case. If it seems to you that your plan would result in an intolerable situation, modify it a little. Or a lot. Go back to the beginning and choose an entirely different plan if you decide that what you've been attempting is actually unworkable. That would just be the process of using experience to make an informed choice about your course of action – none of us can do exactly what we like without there sometimes being circum- stances which we would rather avoid and when that looks likely, then we can modify our plans to find something that is more acceptable all round. *That is also how the world works!*

The seventh (and final) question: *What will your life be like when you have achieved your goal?*

This is another place to let your mind run wild! Choose the sort of life you would choose to live right now if you could – keeping it plausible, possible and fair, of course. Don't stint yourself here; make it *really* good, as good as you could ever imagine achieving. Honestly explore every facet of it that you can think of, looking at the downsides as well as the advantages. (For instance, a big house in the county is wonderful but the heating bills and travelling times to get anywhere might not be.) Ask yourself how it would feel after a couple of years, when you'd become used to it all and if the answer – which might be a feeling – is less than 'wonderful', then have another look to see if what you chose is as close as possible to your absolute ideal situation.

No limit

There's no limit to the number of times you can complete this 'planning for success' routine and, in fact, there's much to be gained from going through it at least three times, with a different plan each time. The point of it is to get your neural cells working free from the restriction that depression has placed upon your thoughts in the past. It's a process that finely tunes the Machine that is your brain a little more each time you run through it. It is a fact that the more you stretch your thoughts in your imagination, the more choice you will be able to find in the real world, because every new thought activates a set of neural pathways in the physical brain that had been laying under-used. Maybe even totally dormant. It doesn't matter that it's all in your imagination, since it is a very well-established fact that as far as the brain is concerned, a thought is valid energy. Whether or not it's connected to a reality is unimportant because the brain, remember, doesn't make any judgement at all as to reality, or good or bad.

It's even possible that one of your success plans will turn into a reality...

The real secret

You've read about this concept earlier but because the idea can be so seductive, it's worth a 'rerun'. There is much persuasive information around these days about 'secret' ways you can get exactly what you want in life without really doing very much to get it. Just read a book, watch a DVD or two, join an online seminar, discover the 'awesome' power of the 'law of attraction', or 'manifestation' or whatever. Well, there is a secret... which is that none of it works in the way it is claimed to!

Yes, there's a grain of truth in the idea that if you visualise strongly enough what you want, believe you deserve it, and truly believe without doubt that it will come to you, you will definitely get it... But it doesn't just drop into your lap or turn up outside your house wrapped up in a gift bow! *You have to **do** something.* There's nothing remarkable about it either – in fact you've already done most of what is necessary. You turned an idea over to your subconscious and wrote down everything it gave you. Writing it down was effectively you taking 'motor action' on what it was doing for you and because you took motor action it gave you even more ideas... Then you took one of those ideas, renamed it to a 'gem' and put it to use in Chapter Thirteen in the 'lite' version of BrainWorking Recursive Therapy®.

Essentially, that's what all the 'secret' concepts do. They teach you how to prime your brain to focus on what you want and give you a torrent of ideas as to how you might achieve your objective. But you still have to take action on the ideas you get. You won't get the sports car simply by imagining it – you might, though, find yourself with an idea as to how you might earn enough money to buy it. You won't get the partner of your dreams just by wanting them to appear in front of you – though you might discover that you find the opportunity to acquire the confidence to do something about meeting them. *You have to do something, just as you've been doing throughout this book* – it's the only true way to find success.

Once in a while, somebody just happens to find themselves with exactly what they wanted without having done anything very much to get it – and of course that sort of case is quoted as 'proof' that 'it', whatever it is that's being promoted, actually works. But... it's coincidence, nothing more. You can wait for that to happen, or you can rely on what you've learnt in this book!

Now read on to find out how to get the very best out of the new life you've started carving out for yourself...

The Rest of Your Life

Up until now, the book has focussed mostly on where you are and the sort of place you came from. But these last two chapters change the pace slightly as we start to look where you're going!

It's not enough just to feel good for a little while after you've read this book... It's important to keep the changes you've made and steadily build upon them. Many people will say things like 'It wears off' when talking about any form of self-help or therapy. But they're wrong! It doesn't wear off at all; the truth is that old patterns try to reassert themselves and for good reason, as you will discover. But all you need to do is a simple 'reminder routine' that will help to keep the New You in beautiful, pristine, impressive shape!

Catching slips before they become falls is easy enough that you'll be able to get the best deal out of life and eventually it will all become so absolutely normal that it will seem to you as if the 'old you' was almost a different person. Well... It was, actually!

Chapter Fifteen

Looking after the new you

The new you is now nicely developed and you are probably already beginning to feel the benefits of your work... But it's not yet 'set in stone'. There's still a vulnerability – there can't *not* be after having experienced depression for so long. Your brain can still remember the 'depression neurones' and might fire them up from time to time unless we provide an 'antidote'. Fortunately, this is an easy thing to do!

We'll get to that very shortly but first of all, we're going to have a look at a little mistake that so many people make from time to time. It's not specifically about depression, nor is it to do with any deep personal issues but you will soon recognise how easy it would be to make a similar mistake. It's told in the form of a story here and it's about a situation that you might find familiar...

Bob and Alice decide to have a day out in the country and so they get into their car and just start driving without having any particular destination in mind. Before long, they are in open countryside beneath a clear blue sky, the car roof down, enjoying the freshness of the air and the feeling of total freedom from restriction. They stop for lunch at an old-fashioned inn where they feast on home-cooked food and freshly brewed coffee before continuing on their way. In a little while, they drive over the crest of a hill to find what looks like the entire English countryside is suddenly spread out before them, a sparkling lake glittering in the distance.

"Wow!" Alice breathes, "Let's stop down there for a little while."

They spend the afternoon on the shores of the lake, just watching small shoals of fish in the shallows, enjoying the warmth of the sun on their skin, the silence around them broken only by the occasional fluttering of birds' wings and the soft buzz of insects from time to time.

"This is amazing," Bob sighs. "Idyllic."

Alice agrees. "Fantastic," she says, "The best day I can remember for a very long time."

Time passes, and as the air begins to grow cooler it's time to leave; they decide to take the quick way home and as they join the motorway, a few spots of rain spatter against the windscreen. "We left just in time," Bob observes, switching on the wipers. The few spots rapidly becomes a downpour, and then they find themselves caught in a tailback of traffic, car rear lights stretching away in front of them in an unmoving trail. "For God's sake!" Bob mutters. "Now what?"

Alice scowls. "Oh wonderful!" she exclaims. "You just can't go anywhere without this sort of thing happening! Well that's the whole day ruined! Thank you God!"

Now, of course, the whole day had *not* been ruined – it's very easy to see that from reading the story. Until the traffic jam and the rain the day had been wonderful and nothing had changed – except their mood. And that's the secret. They *could have* focussed on the fact that they'd had a wonderful day even though the journey home was not so good, which would leave them with a good feeling once they got home. Or they could focus on the worst bit, as they did, and maintain the bad mood for ages afterwards. It's a mistake that many people have made in the past and will make in the future... But you have the opportunity to learn to do something different!

So, if a bit of uncomfortable life flares up at some point – and it will, there's no doubt about that – it's only that bit that is uncomfortable. Nothing else has changed. If it was good to begin with, it's still good now. Interestingly, this concept can be used in reverse, too, because focussing on the good feeling that comes from the improvements you make in your life can render everything that went before it relatively unimportant. It will activate the pathways in your brain that are associated with pleasure and if you *feel* better you will *do* better.

There's a simple lesson to all this, related to the 'but reversal' process in Chapter Four: **Whatever you think of last lasts...** *You can even use a very brief phrase as a reminder: Last thoughts last.*

In your mind right now, link that short phrase to the notion that you will always make the thing you like best about any situation the last thought you have on it, before getting on with anything else. It's easy enough; all that was needed in that short story about Bob and Alice, above, was for one of them to say something like: *"Still, we did have a lovely day, didn't we?"*

All of what you've just been reading can be considered as a kind of backup if you need a bit of help from time to time to keep your spirits lifted. After a while, you probably won't need it, because if you've taken everything to heart so far, and are also absorbing what you read here, you will eventually become what is known as a 'self-winder'. What that means is that if you find a setback at some point in your life, you will:

- Automatically ensure that you become constructive instead of indulging in catastrophisation
- Operate the 'but reversal' automatically when and where you need to
- Use the 'breathing thing' (with the colours and sounds) to find the quiet moment of now
- For really difficult situations, find a quiet place for a few minutes of chakra meditation

You can use those and any of the other exercises you've learned in this book – and always be sure to employ the ones you like best because if you like them best, they suit you best. And if you have an absolute favourite amongst them, then that's the one to try first.

You can even use an ultra-rapid version of BrainWorking Recursive Therapy® if you need it, which, although it doesn't compare with what you did in Chapter Thirteen, is still remarkable for it's speed and effectiveness. It can allow you to let go of all sorts of discomfort for a few hours or maybe even for a few days, until you have an opportunity to do a more complete job. Here's how: Focus for a few seconds on whatever is or has been disturbing you (and don't make the mistake of avoiding the very worst bit!) Make it as vivid as you can and zoom in to the absolute crux of the matter, *the* most uncomfortable part of it, just as you did before. Now freeze it, just as you did before but this time, noticing how the discomfort has stopped. Next, make sure you have your lifeline pointing in front of you – just as in Chapter Seven – and dump the frozen memory firmly somewhere behind you. In your mind now, walk forward without even the merest backward glance, knowing that you're leaving that event further and further behind you with every step.

The antidote

Now we come to what is probably the fastest depression antidote of all, as long as you take on board what you're about to read, creating pictures in your mind as you go. If you want to, you can close your eyes for a moment or two every so often to see the images in your mind's eye, or perhaps you might prefer to just think more vividly of them. It *is* important that you absorb it as fully as possible, though there is absolutely no need to attempt to remember it in any detail. It's the fact that it will create important concepts in the very depths of your psyche as you read it that is important, not the words themselves. If you find your mind drifting at some point, that's just a normal part of the exercise for some individuals; if you notice that happening, continue to explore wherever it is your mind is going and when you've exhausted that train of thought, come back to the last place you remember reading. Even if you drift off completely for a while, this will still work; it's something that the author of this book has been using to good effect with clients for more than twenty years.

This story started a very long time ago, so that you might at first think it can have no bearing on your life at all but you will eventually realise exactly why it might be one of the most important stories you have ever heard. Then, you will see that it actually has a great deal to do with you and the way you feel, as well as the way you function in the world and with other people. It all started more than a million years ago. More than three million years ago, in fact, with our earliest ancestors, the first tribes of hominids. They were more like apes than humans and about the only thing you would recognise as similar to us was that they walked on their hind legs, just as we do. But they were natural survivors in a hostile environment, hunting and gathering their food, and competing with other tribes of hominids to maintain their territory. They were able to plan, just as we do today, and would kill their enemies, just as some of us do today, though there's no doubt that they had only the most primitive of weapons to do so, maybe just wielding rocks with their bare hands.

It's fair to say that life was tough and the world totally unforgiving of anybody who was not properly alert or who failed to keep their wits about them and their mind on the task of surviving. The best amongst them were astonishingly shrewd and more naturally skilled, so that they lived longer and produced more offspring. Their children, of course, had inherited those superior genes for success and in turn would learn to hunt even more efficiently and effectively than their fathers. And so each generation passed on their skills to the next; it was always the fittest and strongest who thrived, who passed their skills and genes on to the next generation. They in turn became even fitter and stronger, while the weakest gradually faded into the obscurity which is the destination for all species which are not perfectly adapted to their environment.

It all carried on for thousands upon thousands of years, the genes for the best opportunity for success and survival being passed on to each successive generation. If you can, think of two streams of genetic information being passed on from parent to child in different parts of the world, perhaps associated with two different tribes, but each carrying the perfect blueprint for human survival in the most hostile of worlds. The tribes might have been separated by thousands of miles, yet each carried those perfectly formed survival instincts in their own pure line that was everything that man was designed to be. Over the years there were huge earthquakes, flood and tempest, massive volcanic eruptions, pestilence, plagues and horrendous famine, and yet still these two streams of genetic information survived. The individuals who were carrying them defeated incredible odds against survival, passing on those by now highly developed genes for success to their children... and those children survived unheard of before wars and dreadful inventions like guns, bombs, warships and rockets.

*And then, one day just a little while before you were born, the two individuals who were carrying these ancestral genes came together in a single moment in time. And in that single moment, **you** were created! **You** are now the bearer of the strengths they had carried with them, the bearer of a magnificent and completely unique genetic stream. It's a genetic code that carries with it the resources and skills that our ancestors developed and nurtured over millions of years, and all those skills are now yours as a gift from ancient history. You couldn't **not** have them because they are your birthright and they are responsible for your very existence.*

And this might seem like an awesome thought as you realise that you are totally unique and yet the equal of any other because we are all totally unique. It's an absolute truth that every one of us is in some way special, and even though you may sometimes recognise that you feel different from how others seem, it is an inescapable fact that you have inherited those genetic instincts for success and survival. It means that whatever situations you experience in the world, you have the resources to deal with them as well as they can be dealt with. And just as your ancestors did, you can easily turn a setback into an advantage if you put your mind to it, because you have every ability possible to do such a thing, even if it doesn't always feel like it.

Now, we haven't got to the clever bit yet – that comes next – but before we do it is important that you've understood the absolute enormity of what you've just been reading. There's nothing ficti-tious about it; you can try to find flaws and errors in the idea if you like but the fact is you *are* descended from those ancient people whose survival depended upon their resources and skills, and you have inherited those genes for success. When you're certain you've grasped that, maybe even feeling a little in awe of your inheritance, you're ready to move on to the clever part that's going to give you a tool for an instant elevation of your self-worth whenever you need it:

*First imagine an enormous sheet of paper, perhaps the size of a football pitch – so big anyway that you really can't see all of it at once. At the top left is an image of one of your ancestors from millions of years ago – and make that vivid in your mind now in any way you can; and at the top right, is another one of your ancestors from the other tribe, and again, make that image really vivid. Now imagine you can see the chains of ancestors slowly moving down the paper, their strengths and resources being handed on to the next generation in each link of the chain. Imagine the two lines drawing gradually closer together until they join at the bottom of that massive sheet, forming a huge 'V'. And that's where **you** are – at the point of those millions of years of your ancestors' survival. Now imagine that huge sheet of paper beginning to shrink, shrinking faster and faster until it's just about the size and thickness of a credit card. It has a simple 'V' printed on it but you know **exactly** what that 'V' stands for...*

It stands for everything that you are and everything you can be.

It stands for everything you will ever need in life and everything you can do. It stands for the resources to solve life's problems whenever they arise and to solve them so easily and so effectively that you recognise that you could always do this. In your mind, now, see the colour of that V and the thickness and texture of the card. And whenever you need a bit of a boost, whatever that boost may be, all you need to do is to hold a vivid image of that V in your mind for a moment or two and you will suddenly find everything that you need in order to be able to do whatever you need to do.

If you want to add an even more powerful resource to this concept, you can create a physical card about the size of a credit card, print or draw a 'V' that reaches from the corners to the bottom and keep it with you all the time. When you need it, just holding the point of the 'V' between your finger and thumb will have a hugely beneficial effect upon your well-being.

The first aid kit

In the final section of this chapter, you have the opportunity to create a personal 'first aid kit', a collection of your favourite instant exercises from the book. Not everything is suitable, since some of the routines involve a fair bit of writing and are not really ideal for a first aid situation. To create your kit, you'll choose the six routines you like best, write them down on a small card (it can be the other side of the 'V' card) so that at any time you need to give yourself an instant fix you can take it out and decide which routine, or routines, is relevant for both the situation and the circumstances in which you find yourself. Here's a list of the exercises – they include some of those you encountered at the beginning of Chapter Eight:

- The Double-sided Cheval Mirror (Chapter One)
- The 'Act of Will' (Chapter Two)
- The Smile and the High Five (Chapter Two

- The Deadly Embrace test (Chapter Three)
- The 'Breathing Thing' (Chapter Four)
- 'But Reversal' (Chapter Four)
- The Virtual World (Chapter Four)
- The "Wait a Minute!" Solution (Chapter Five)
- The Locked Safe (Chapter Five)
- Exercising the Favourite Aspect of Personality (Chapter Six)
- The VMI Exercises (Chapter Six)
- The Lifeline Exercise (Chapter Seven)
- Parts Apart (Chapter Ten)
- Freedom (Chapter Eleven)
- Can't Versus Won't (Chapter Eleven)
- Chakra Meditation (Chapter Twelve)
- BrainWorking Recursive Therapy® (Chapter Thirteen)
- The Machine (Chapter Fourteen – not an exercise but a contemplation)
- Planning for Success (Chapter Fourteen)
- The V Card (this Chapter)
- Ultra-rapid BrainWorking Recursive Therapy® (this Chapter)

There are nineteen ideas to choose from and each of them has a specific purpose, so the ones you choose as your first aid kit are likely to be those that are most relevant to the way you function. Some of them are more important than others though and would ideally be chosen for everybody's kit. In particular, these are:

The breathing thing: This is allows a rapid calm down from anxiety (not unusual with depression) or an easy way to take a calm look at any uncomfortable situation. It can be done anywhere you can find a quiet place for a couple of minutes – even a public toilet is a possibility and is a great way of coping with tricky situations. It can also be used to enhance some of the other exercises, such as **The Lifeline, Freedom** and either of the **VMI Exercises.**

The Ultra-Rapid BrainWorking Recursive Therapy®: This is excellent for dealing with the sudden unexpected assault on your sensibilities. We're not talking about a genuine assault here, of course, but about your own reaction to something uncomfortable. With practice, you can render it completely impotent, whatever it is, for long enough that you can continue with your day, perhaps working through the problem more completely later on.

The VMI Exercise: You don't need to go through the whole thing of creating the image again, of course (though you could if you feel they might have changed.) All you need here is your three-word description of yourself that you created in Chapter Six, then you can carry out a rapid, yet powerful procedure that can be done in seconds when you get used to it. It's ideal for when you have to deal with an uncomfortable circumstance. All you need to do is visualise each VMI being in charge of the situation and see which feels best. Having got that, you hold the relevant VMI in your mind for just a few seconds when you need it (just before you have to deal with the situation is ideal) and this will condition your brain to find the right neural patterns to handle it. This is one of those situations where it's useful to remember what Benjamin Libet discovered in 1983 – the brain makes our decisions before we know about it, so prime it and let it get on with it!

So those three techniques would form the basis of an excellent first aid kit that you could use on a daily basis if you needed to. In practice, though, you will find yourself using them less and less frequently as you grow in confidence and your depression becomes a thing of the past. You might be a little doubtful about the possibility of that at this stage and that is a perfectly 'normal' reaction. But it *is* possible and many people have done it before you. Self-belief is everything, so remember the 'V' card to bolster you when you need it (though that one is so easy, it doesn't actually have to be part of your first aid kit.) Of course, if you wanted to add more than six routines you can do so but the snag is that it can take longer to decide which to use – and that can increase stress.

Once you've compiled your kit, it's a good idea to decide which is going to be your primary methodology, the thing you will drift to instantly if something catches you by surprise. You might discover that you can use just the most important part of it within a second or two – for instance, taking just the 'freeze' moment from the **BrainWorking Recursive Therapy**® technique. Many people have discovered that all they need to do is feel the discomfort, think about the freeze, and they can just lay it to one side to work at more thoroughly later on. That can be done in less than ten seconds!

And that's the last part of this book that is about fixing your depression directly – but don't put it down yet because there's still one more chapter to go, one which is just as important as anything you've read so far. It's all about a technique used by millions of people all over the world to enhance their lives, achieve their goals, and make powerful changes within themselves with next to no effort. It's not some 'secret mystical concept' but something which has been used for thousands of years and has even now been accepted in the scientific world as being a useful adjunct to conventional medicine.

Turn the page to find out more and see how it might turn out to be the 'icing on the cake' for you!

Chapter Sixteen

The astonishing effectiveness of self-hypnosis

Now, before you run off screaming that you want nothing to do with hypnosis or anything like it; do at least read on for a little while. After all, just reading what is written here cannot suddenly hurl you into some mystical 'trance' of some sort can it?

It's not unknown for people to fear they might get somehow 'stuck' in the state of self-hypnosis – or any form of hypnosis, come to that. But this is simply not possible, any more than getting stuck watching a film is; although you might not realise it, watching a film *does* create a state of mild hypnosis. This is why, if you are totally engrossed in what you are looking at, two specific things might happen:

- You don't hear other stuff going on around you.
- You bypass credibility and get emotionally involved with fictitious events on the screen as if they were real – but you know they're not.

In fact, hypnosis is nothing more than a total focus on an idea or concept, just like watching a film... or reading a book. Even this book. Nobody ever got stuck in hypnosis and just as you can decide to stop watching a film or reading a book when you want to, so you can leave the state of hypnosis the moment you decide to do so. Not only that, but an individual in hypnosis is well aware of everything going on around them the whole time (there is no loss of conscious awareness), though most stage hypnotists might try to convince you otherwise. After all, it would rather spoil the fun if you realised that those on the stage knew perfectly well what they were doing but simply saw no reason to not do it! It's worth the recognition that those the stage hypnotist selects to work with are all volunteers who know exactly the sort of thing they might be asked to do; they're evidently 'up for it' or they wouldn't volunteer in the first place.

So, in a nutshell, hypnosis *allows* an individual to do something they might have had difficulty doing otherwise but it cannot *make* them do anything they don't want to. It is a very well-established truth that if an attempt is made to make somebody do something they don't want to, they will exit the state of hypnosis immediately – so that's not really much of a mind-control method! The stuff you sometimes see in films, where a hypnotist only has to look at somebody in a certain way, snap their fingers, or utter a trigger word to have their 'subject' fall hopelessly under some kind of spell... All bunk. They're just there for dramatic entertainment, usually because the writers haven't researched properly, and are instead just regurgitating what they *imagine* hypnosis is and what it can do. Those things *can* create the state of hypnosis but they will only be able to do so if the 'hypnotisee' is a totally willing participant in the process and agrees to go along with it. Hypnosis is a purely voluntary state – if somebody doesn't want to enter it, they won't. It's as simple as that.

Now, that other old myth, that some people's minds are just 'too strong' to allow them to be hypnotised... More bunk. It's a fact that the stronger the mind, the easier it is to get into hypnosis, because it's all about being able to combine concentration and imagination. Not being hypnotisable is actually an indicator of fear, misunderstanding, or the inability to focus concentration or imagination. Nothing to boast about there! There are only two problems with hypnosis, neither of them serious or insurmountable:

1.   It doesn't actually feel like anything. Most people will say afterwards that they just felt 'normal' and that they could easily have opened their eyes at any time.

2. Hypnosis doesn't happen at all if it's being tested for. So if somebody keeps on investigating to see if they feel different in some way, they won't get into hypnosis. They just have to trust that they will.

It's possible that you might have seen somebody apparently unable to open their eyes, forgetting a number, 'levitating' their arm, or some other trick; these are all the product of suggestion applied after the state of hypnosis has been induced. Even then, though, it's not at all what it seems. If there were a sudden *need* to open their eyes, remember the number or use their arm, the exit from the suggestion would be immediate and certainly wouldn't need the help of the hypnotist. Hypnotic suggestion can be very powerful, provided the suggestion is for something you truly *want* to happen; it can even be used sometimes for control of discomfort and pain in quite major operations without any chemical anaesthetic – though the hypnotist is usually on standby to deepen the state if necessary.

So, professional hypnosis is all about *giving* a person control, not taking it away from them. It's all about tuning the mind to be able to help do anything which is plausible, possible and fair – it couldn't make an olympic sprinter out of a sixty-year old individual but it could help that individual to become as fit and as fast as it was possible for them to be, for instance. It would be unlikely to turn a retiring introvert into an extrovert super salesman but it could enhance their confidence and well-being sufficiently for them to become completely comfortable 'in their own skin'.

You're probably getting the idea by now, and hopefully have come to the conclusion that there's nothing to fear, in which case we can get onto the important 'business' of this final chapter – providing you with one of the best self-help tools that ever existed! *The author of this book has been using hypnosis to help people for more than twenty-five years at the time of writing (2014) and so is well-qualified to help you discover just how easy it is to get into a state of self-hypnosis and exit again when you want to.*

How does it work?

That's the thousand-dollar-question! As unlikely as it seems, nobody really understands exactly why hypnosis is able to do what it clearly does, especially when it comes to controlling the pain of major surgery. What *is* known is that while almost everybody can get into some state of hypnosis, some people seem to be a lot better than others at learning how to do it. There are some who are completely natural; get them into hypnosis just once and they can take themselves into the deepest of possible states almost immediately. And yet others find they cannot ever achieve anything other than an eyes-closed relaxed state – though whatever state a person can achieve can still be used to good purpose.

It's possible that it works by creating an intense focus on the single subject at hand so that nothing else can interfere with the idea; in this way, the brain perceives it as a matter of some importance and therefore sets out to achieve it. The problem with that solution, though, is that it doesn't answer the question of how it works to prevent or block pain... or give an athlete the ability to run faster, jump higher, or throw something further than ever before. It doesn't quite explain how it allows an individual to quit a lifelong habit literally overnight with no withdrawal symptoms (though not usually with hard drugs like heroin). There are many other examples that deny explanation and so all you can do is to accept the simple truth that although nobody really knows how or why, it definitely works!

Who does it best?

There's no doubt that your basic personality determines, to an extent, how easily you can learn to get into hypnosis – for instance, a cynical and sceptical individual might never learn it and be insistent that it was all a fake. On the other hand, a creative and curious person would be likely to learn it very easily and wonder why on earth anybody would have difficulty with it.

You can probably remember what your dominant personality trait is (from Chapter Six) out of Warrior, Nomad and Settler... Well, in general, the **Nomad** personality fares best with hypnosis; the **Settler** can do well as long as they don't worry about it; but the **Warrior** has to learn the trick of not testing it if they want to get the best results. Even if it didn't work as well as you hoped, though, it is still impossible to create harm and the worst thing that would happen is that you didn't get a particularly remarkable result.

How do you do it?

We'll get on to the process of actually getting into hypnosis in a little while but first, there's something that is much more important to understand, and that is what you will actually *do* while you're there. Hypnosis on its own will achieve nothing at all – you need a **hypnotic suggestion** to do the actual work of the session. This has to be formulated in a very specific way to say *exactly* what you want. Not what you don't want: *"I don't want to feel depressed any more,"* says nothing about what you *do* want and so your brain would do nothing. The phrase: *"From now on, I want to feel completely comfortable with who I am,"* says all that is needed for constructive change to take place. So does: *"From now on, I will find it so easy to do things for myself,"* though it would be even better if those 'things' were clearly defined. You would repeat these suggestions to yourself several times once in the state of hypnosis and they will have more strength if you link them to a 'mental video clip' that you would see in your mind's eye – that's rather like some of the work you've done in other exercises in this book, so you'll probably find it easy.

So, your first task is to write down exactly what you want to happen – and do choose just one thing! Although it's possible to work on more than one thing at a time, that's really the domain of the professional therapist. If you're finding it difficult to define what you want, then you can choose something from this list of 'affirmations' which are essentially small suggestions. Now, you *can* add two or three of those together to make one concept or suggestion if you like. Here's the list, taken from the author's website at http://www.hypnosense.com

1. I find it easy to discard negative thoughts and attitudes about myself
2. I always think of myself in a totally positive way
3. I expect to succeed because I am a naturally successful person
4. I am tenacious and persevere with all my efforts towards success
5. I quickly see and use all opportunities for success
6. My naturally successful personality ensures my natural success
7. I find it easy to achieve my goals and I set my goals high
8. I move steadily and single-mindedly towards my chosen goals
9. I become steadily more confident with each day that passes
10. I am a worthwhile and loveable person
11. I am my own person, the equal of all others; nobody controls me
12. I face fears and responsibilities with confidence
13. I am a natural optimist. I expect things to work out well, and they do
14. I naturally move towards solutions rather than away from problems
15. I make decisions quickly and my decisions are correct because of this
16. I am always relaxed and assured in everything I do
17. I enjoy meeting people because people enjoy meeting me

18. I possess great energy; the more I use it, the more I have
19. I am naturally enthusiastic and enthusiasm gives me energy
20. I am a natural optimist; I can always turn a setback to an advantage
21. I am a dynamic person and I pursue my goals energetically
22. I always think of what I actually want to happen
23. I always think of how I want to be
24. I look forward to beneficial change and I enjoy beneficial change
25. I do everything that is necessary to achieve my goals

Select what feels most relevant to you from that list and if you're going to use them in combination, be sure they work. For instance, numbers 2, 10 and 16 are good together: *"I always think of myself in a totally positive way* because *I am a worthwhile and loveable person* and *I am always relaxed and assured in everything I do."* You can see how they create a positive concept; if it's a bit long for your liking, then you could use any two of those three together and they'll still make perfect sense. Now we need to make one other change and that is to convert them to the third person because experiments have shown that hypnosis works better that way. So you would get: *"You always think of yourself in a totally positive way because you are a worthwhile and loveable person and you are always relaxed and assured in everything you do."*

So read through them now, find the ones you like best, and create the first hypnotic suggestion you will be using for yourself very shortly!

The self-hypnosis session

Although you might not have realised it, you have already done quite a bit of preparation for this, with the 'breathing thing' and the Chakra meditation. It's true that hypnosis and meditation is not the same thing, but there are certain similarities and you could use either meditation routine for fifteen minutes or so before the suggestion work if you wish. Also, if you feel like it, you can have some soft music playing in the background.

When it comes to delivering the suggestion, you have three choices:

1. Think it to yourself with a vivid impression of the 'mental video', being sure to use 'you' rather than 'I'. Do it six times.
2. Say it aloud to yourself in the same way.
3. Record it to start around fifteen minutes after the beginning of your session, repeating it half-a-dozen times or so, going quite slowly but with some 'colour' to give it energy.

When you've finished with the suggestion, there's no need to rush to the end of the session – you can enjoy the sense of calmness and relaxation that most people discover for a while. Do be aware, though, that there is often a peculiar 'time distortion' effect in hypnosis, so that what feels like only ten minutes might actually be half-an-hour or more. Not everybody experiences this, and the only way to find out if you do is by experiment – the first session will tell you and you might have already discovered it via the 'breathing thing' and/or the meditation.

Of course, if you record the suggestion, you will know that fifteen minutes have passed at that time. This will make it easier to judge the total length of the session, and when you're ready to leave it, just count up to five *very slowly* in your mind, then open your eyes. Once in a while, you might find yourself with a slightly 'muzzy' feeling at this point, a sensation known as 'hypnotic hangover' – but this is nothing of concern; just close your eyes again and count up to five once more, going even more slowly and visualise yourself becoming more alert with every count.

The professional method

If you want to use self-hypnosis in the most professional way possible, this is actually very easy to do, though you will need some extra preparation. You can either record the script that's presented here, using a fairly monotone and low-ish voice at about 130 words per minute, or you can learn the concept and run through it in your mind, which is the way that a professional would do it and is possibly the most effective method. You would first do the 'breathing thing', or the meditation, (which you could also record, of course) then continue straight away with this tried and tested 'deepener' script used by many professional hypnotherapists all over the world:

"Now you can begin to imagine, as vividly as you can, that you are at the top of a beautiful, warm, softly-lit staircase with ten steps to go down... all covered in a beautifully soft carpet in your favourite colour and design... with a wonderfully smooth hardwood handrail at the side. At the bottom of the staircase is a door, and behind the door is a room, your own special room, where nobody ever goes but you... in a moment or two, I'm going to count all the way down from ten down to zero... and as I count all the way down from ten, down to zero... you can imagine that each number is a step on this staircase... another step down into deeper and deeper levels of relaxation... so that by the time I get to zero... you will be as relaxed as you can ever be...

10... take the first step down now, plenty of time, no need to hurry.
9... feeling more and more relaxed, moving down easily.
8... another step down now, into a relaxed calmness.
7... imagining how it feels as your hand glides down that stair rail.
6... going deeper now... deeper.
5... feeling more and more relaxed.
4... deeper still now... and still deeper.
3... your breathing becoming slower now... and steadier.

2.. a wonderful calmness just sweeping over you.
1...almost all the way down now... just one more step to go, to...
0... zero...

And now you find yourself in front of that door to your own special room; study it for a moment, noticing the colour and design, looking at the texture and pattern of the handle and understand that this room is always here for you in your thoughts... you can always find it just by going down that staircase of calmness and relaxation in your mind. Then you open the door and move easily inside the room. It's comfortable and warm inside here, and softly lit, and furnished exactly as you want it to be to make it absolutely perfect... make it truly vivid in your mind, catching the smell of it, the feel of it... as well as the way it looks... because this is a room where you can make wonderful things happen for yourself, just by imagining them... in the middle of the room is a comfortable chair, the most luxurious and comfortable chair you have ever seen... and you just dawdle lazily over to it and flop yourself down, marvelling at the deep sense of tranquillity that sweeps over you...as you... just relax... nobody wanting anything...nobody expecting anything...allowing yourself to become more relaxed than you can ever remember. And your subconscious mind is now ready and prepared to accept the suggestions I'm going to give you... and nothing that's accepted into subconscious is easily removed, so you can be certain that they'll be there, helping you, guiding you, over the coming days and weeks and months... helping you and guiding you to achieve your wishes and desires, and achieving those things so easily that you become the envy of others..."

And this is where you would read, say or think the suggestion that you've already created for yourself, repeating it six or so times, then just allowing a few moments before ending the session:

"That's good... And now it's time to bring the session to an end, so in your mind now, just get up lazily from the comfortable chair and

move towards the door... The door opens for you as you approach and you notice that it closes gently behind you as you make your way to the foot of the stairs, those ten steps stretching up in front of you... And as I count from one, all the way up to ten now, you find yourself becoming more and more alert with each step you take... So that by the time I get to ten, you will find yourself wide awake, alert and feeling good...

1...*Take the first step now, already feeling more aware*
2... *Step two now moving upwards so easily*
3... *As you take this step you feel a sense of achievement somewhere*
4... *Further up now, become more alert with every moment*
5...*Pausing half way up to thank your subconscious for listening today*
6... *Really beginning to feel an energy about you now*
7... *Moving steadily upwards to full awareness*
8... *You can feel energy in your body now*
9... *Almost all the way up to the top behind your closed eyelids*
10... *And all the way up now, eyes open, and feeling great!*

At this point, you might decide to just relax for a little while longer, or on the other hand, you might feel so energised that you simply can't wait to get started on the rest of your day!

What next?

Well, most people who know how to do it practise self-hypnosis on a daily basis but it won't be long before you don't need any of the script work at all. Just as you practised finding the 'quiet moment of now' without going through the 'breathing thing' first, so when you know exactly what hypnosis feels like *to you* (because it feels different to everybody, *if* it has any feeling at all) you can just drop into the state, sometimes in just a few seconds. That won't happen at first though and in any case, doing the full routine every day for a while will really get that subconscious mind of yours working for you instead of against you as it has done so many times in the past.

And now you're at the beginning of an entirely new phase in your life, a place from where you can choose to develop yourself pretty much as you wish, with a variety of tools to help you on your way.

Be sure to enjoy the journey!

A Little Extra

In case you need professional help

If you feel that this book hasn't quite done for you what you wanted it to, don't give up! Having made a lot of effort here, you will have at least put the processes of change in motion and to complete the task you can search out a professional therapist to help you. If you have a healthcare programme in your country (such as the National Health Service in the UK) then you should approach your general practitioner and request an appointment with a psychotherapist. Waiting lists can be quite long and it's likely that you will be prescribed medication in the meantime – which is not at all a bad idea and can even help the work you have done with this book, to 'take'. Also, keep on working with that first aid kit that you created.

If you want to find help in the private sector, then it's worth investigating psychotherapy, counselling and hypnotherapy. Just typing those terms into any search engine will find you many associations and organisations from which to select a therapist – and do be sure to find one who specialises in depression. Not all of them do and it is a specialist area.

Finally, for self-help and lots of other interesting 'stuff', you can visit the website of the author of this and many other books: www.hypnosense.com

Terence Watts, 2014

Resources

There is no claim that the organisations listed here are preferred or in some way better than others, only that they are known to be reputable.

Counselling (BACP): http://www.bacp.co.uk/
Psychotherapy (UKCP): http://www.psychotherapy.org.uk
Hypnotherapy: http://www.hypnotherapy-directory.org.uk
The Complementary and Natural Healthcare Council:
http://www.cnhc.org.uk
Meridian therapy: http://theamt.com
Cognitive Behavioural Therapy (CBT):
http://www.mind.org.uk/mental_health_a-z/8000_cognitive
_behaviour_therapy

Some private organisations that might be helpful:

The following are known to be reputable associations of therapists in the UK that have a strict code of ethics to which their members must adhere:

The Association for Professional Hypnosis and Psychotherapy:
http://www.aphp.co.uk
The National Register of Psychotherapists and Counsellors
Http://www.nrpc.co.uk
The National Council for Hypnotherapy:
http://www.hypnotherapists.org.uk
WSN-counselling and Coaching
Http://www.wsn-counselling.co.uk

Bibliography

Depressive Illness (2006) Christopher Cantopher, Sheldon Press, London, UK

The Depression Book (1999) Cheri Huber, Keep it Simple Books, USA

Managing Depression with CBT for Dummies (2012), Brian Thomson, Matt Broadway-Horner, John a Wiley and Sons

Warriors, Settlers & Nomads (2000) Terence Watts, Crown House, Swansea, UK

Rapid Cognitive Therapy (1999) Terence Watts and Georges Phillips, Crown House, Swansea, UK

The Psychopathology of Everyday Life (orig. 1901, first British ed. 1914) Freud, Penguin Books, London

The Professional Practitioner Training Course (1999 – 2014) Terence Watts

Other books by Terence Watts

The Secret Life of Love and Sex
Rapid Cognitive Therapy
Warriors, Settlers & Nomads
HYPNOSIS: Advanced Techniques in Hypnosis and Hypnoanalysis
Magic! for Minds
7 Ways and 7 Days to Banish Your Anxiety
Various professional text books